ASIAN POLITICAL, ECONOMIC AND SECURITY ISSUES

INDIA AND MALAYSIA

SERVICE SECTOR GROWTH

ASIAN POLITICAL, ECONOMIC AND SECURITY ISSUES

Additional books in this series can be found on Nova's website
under the Series tab.

Additional E-books in this series can be found on Nova's website
under the E-book tab.

TRADE ISSUES, POLICIES AND LAWS

Additional books in this series can be found on Nova's website
under the Series tab.

Additional E-books in this series can be found on Nova's website
under the E-book tab.

INDIA AND MALAYSIA

SERVICE SECTOR GROWTH

SAMIR ORUJOV

AND

SOUTA MORI

EDITORS

Nova Science Publishers, Inc.

New York

NOTICE TO THE READER

Library of Congress Cataloging-in-Publication Data
India and Malaysia : service sector growth / editors, Samir Orujov and Souta Mori.
    p. cm. -- (Asian political, economic and security issues) (Trade issues, policies and laws)
  Includes bibliographical references and index.
  ISBN 978-1-61470-508-6 (hardcover)
  1. Service industries--India. 2. Service industries--Malaysia. I. Orujov, Samir. II. Mori, Souta. III. United States International Trade Commission. IV. Series: Asian political, economic and security issues. V. Series: Trade issues, policies and laws series.
  HD9987.I42I53 2011   338.40954--dc23   2011024415

Published by Nova Science Publishers, Inc. † New York

CONTENTS

PREFACE

This book examines the service sector growth of both India and Malaysia. India's service sector has grown rapidly since the 1990s. Domestic demand for services has increased as incomes have risen, triggering the expansion of industries such as banking, education and telecommunications. Exports have also increased rapidly, led by information technology and business process outsourcing (IT-BPO). India's ability to offer low-cost, high quality IT-BPO services has made it a world leader in this industry. The growing global competitiveness of Malaysia's service sector is reflected in steady growth in trade volumes. Malaysia's cross-border trade in services increased at an average annual rate of 15 percent to $60.6 billion from 2004 through 2008, accounting for 13 percent of total Malaysian cross-border trade and about 1 percent of global services trade in 2008.

Chapter 1- Between 2001 and 2008, U.S. imports of services from India grew at a compound annual growth rate of 31 percent—faster than from any other country. India's service exports have contributed significantly to the country's economic growth, and the growth of service industries has been a driving force for poverty reduction. This chapter examines the service sector of this increasingly important trading partner. It is the first in a series of studies of services in important emerging economies.

Chapter 2- The service sector is a large and growing component of Malaysia's expanding economy, accounting for almost 55 percent of that country's gross domestic product (GDP) and approximately 13 percent of total Malaysian cross-border trade in 2008. A significant part of the Malaysian government's current economic strategy is aimed at improving the competitiveness of the Malaysian service sector, with dedicated programs to encourage domestic and foreign investment in certain service industries and increase these industries' productivity. Malaysia is one of Asia's key service markets, given its ties with regional partners, including members of the Association of Southeast Asian Nations (ASEAN); its significant overall bilateral trade relationship with the United States; its status as the site of significant U.S. foreign investment; and its ongoing negotiations with the United States in pursuit of a bilateral free trade agreement (FTA).

In: India and Malaysia: Service Sector Growth   ISBN: 978-1-61470-508-6
Editors: Samir Orujov, Souta Mori   © 2012 Nova Science Publishers, Inc.

Chapter 1

AN OVERVIEW AND EXAMINATION OF THE INDIAN SERVICES SECTOR[*]

Lisa Alejandro, Eric Forden, Allison Gosney,
Erland Herfindahl, Dennis Luther,
Erick Oh, Joann Peterson, Matthew Reisman,
and Isaac Wohl[†]

ABSTRACT

India's service sector has grown rapidly since the 1990s. Domestic demand for services has increased as incomes have risen, triggering the expansion of industries such as banking, education, and telecommunications. Exports have also increased rapidly, led by information technology and business process outsourcing (IT-BPO). India's ability to offer low-cost, high-quality IT-BPO services has made it a world leader in this industry. However, employment in services has not grown as quickly as output. The majority of India's jobseekers are low-skilled, but demand for workers is growing fastest in higher-skill

---

[*] This is an edited, reformatted and augmented version of a United States International Trade Commission publication No. ID-26, dated August 2010.

[†] The authors wish to thank Karen Laney, Linda Linkins, Richard Brown, Robert Feinberg, William Powers, Jennifer Powell, Margaret Hausman, and Samantha Brady for their comments and Patricia M. Thomas and Cynthia Payne for their assistance.

industries. The supply of highly-skilled workers has not kept pace with demand, causing wages to increase faster for these workers than for lower-skilled ones.

India's government has supported the growth of service industries through a mix of deregulation, liberalization, and incentive programs, such as the Software Technology Parks of India. Nevertheless, burdensome regulations, poor infrastructure, and foreign investment restrictions continue to affect service firms' ability to do business. USITC analysis suggests that additional liberalization would lead to an increase in India's imports of services.

INTRODUCTION

Between 2001 and 2008, U.S. imports of services from India grew at a compound annual growth rate of 31 percent—faster than from any other country.[1] India's service exports have contributed significantly to the country's economic growth, and the growth of service industries has been a driving force for poverty reduction.[2] This paper examines the service sector of this increasingly important trading partner. It is the first in a series of studies of services in important emerging economies.[3]

Part I examines the contribution of services to the Indian economy, describes India's participation in international trade in services, reviews the liberalization of India's service sector, and explores the potential effects of future liberalization. An original analysis by Commission staff suggests that India's imports of services could increase by as much as 47 percent if India were to relax most of its restrictions on foreign participation in the sector.

Part II profiles six Indian service industries: information technology and business process outsourcing (IT-BPO),[4] telecommunications, energy, air transport, education, and financial services. A concluding section suggests areas in which future research is especially vital. The paper focuses on the past ten years, but includes data from earlier periods in order to highlight important changes in specific industries or in the service sector as a whole.

PART I: OVERVIEW OF THE INDIAN SERVICES SECTOR

Services in the Indian Economy

In 2008, India's services sector accounted for 53 percent of the country's GDP, higher than in certain other lower-middle-income countries, such as China (40 percent), Indonesia (37 percent), and Thailand (43 percent), and higher than the average share recorded for all countries in this income category (45 percent).[5] Value added in India's services sector grew by 10 percent in 2008, equal to such growth in China, but higher than the growth recorded in the service sectors of other lower-middle-income countries, including Indonesia (9 percent), the Philippines (3 percent), and Thailand (5 percent).[6] Growth in India's services sector accelerated rapidly in the 1990s, eventually outpacing growth in the country's agricultural and industrial sectors (table 1).[7]

Table 1. Annual growth rates in India's agriculture, manufacturing and services sectors, 1985–2008

Sector	1985	1990	1995	2000	2005	2008	Compound annual growth rate, 1985–2008
Agriculture	0	4	-1	0	6	3	3
Manufacturing	3	5	15	8	9	4	6
Services	8	5	10	6	11	10	8

Source: World Bank, WDI Online Database (accessed August 9, 2010). The data measure annual growth of value added in each sector, based on constant local currency.

Despite the relatively rapid rise of the Indian services sector in the past two decades, growth within the sector has been uneven. Service industries that experienced the largest growth during this period include banking, business (including computer services), communication, education, healthcare, and tourism services. By comparison, the distribution and transportation services industries grew at a more modest pace. Reasons for this mixed growth among India's service industries include changes in the composition of services demand in the domestic economy beginning in the 1990s, and the increasing importance of information technology, which enabled India's business services industry to grow at a faster rate than all other service industries during the period.[8] Overall, in 2007, wholesale and retail trade accounted for the largest share of Indian services GDP (24 percent), followed by community, social, and personal services (22 percent); transport, storage, and communication (14 percent); real estate and business services (13 percent); and construction (13 percent) (figure 1).[9]

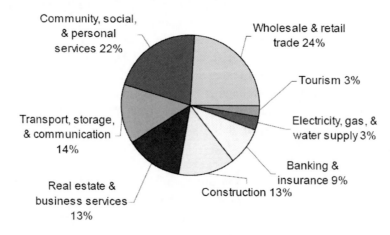

Total: $50 billion

Source: Government of India, Ministry of Statistics and Programme Implementation, Central Statistical Organization, National Accounts Statistics, 2006–07 , May 2009, 75. Industry shares do not sum to 100 due to rounding.

Figure 1. Wholesale and retail trade account for the largest proportion of GDP in India's services sector.

In 2005, the latest year for which data are available, the services sector accounted for approximately 30 percent of total employment, compared to 58 percent and 12 percent in the agricultural and manufacturing sectors, respectively.[10]

Industries that accounted for the largest shares of Indian services employment were wholesale and retail trade (35 percent); community, social and personal services (27 percent); and construction services (19 percent) (figure 2). GDP growth in India's services sector has not been accompanied by commensurate growth in employment, a phenomenon that has been characterized as "jobless growth."[11] For instance, during the period 1991–2001, employment in India's services sector increased by only 1 percent, whereas the sector's contribution to GDP increased by roughly 6 percent. In general, services' share of employment appears to be far lower in India than in other countries where the sector accounts for a similar proportion of GDP. For example, while in India the services sector accounts for 53 percent of total GDP and 30 percent of total employment, in Malaysia, the services sector accounts for 51 percent of GDP and 55 percent of the country's total employment, and in the Philippines, it accounts for 54 percent of GDP and 48 percent of employment.[12]

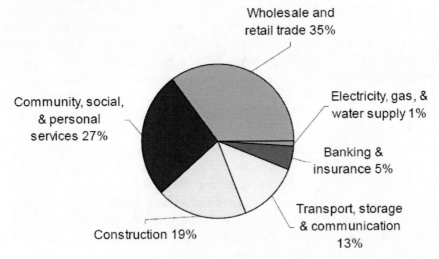

Total: 134.5 million employees

Source: IndiaStat, "Employed Workers in Selected Industrys [sic] in India" (accessed August 3, 2009). Data are for 2004–05.

[a] The source used for these calculations does not provide data for several service industries, such as tourism and real estate and business services.

Figure 2. Wholesale and retail trade account for the largest share of service sector employment in India.[a]

The relatively slow growth of employment in services reflects the fact that the sector's growth has been led by industries that depend heavily on highly-skilled labor and in which labor productivity is high, such as banking, information technology, [13] and telecommunications.[14] Service industries that depend heavily on unskilled labor and in which labor productivity is lower, such as retail trade,[15] have not grown as quickly.

Factors Affecting Demand

Growth in the demand for Indian services has been influenced by India's growing middle class and by a sharp rise in business process outsourcing (BPO) by foreign and domestic firms. Growth in India's middle class, as evidenced by increasing GDP per capita, has increased domestic demand for consumer-oriented services such as healthcare, education, telecommunications, and tourism.[16] For example, household expenditures on private healthcare services, which are perceived to be of higher quality than public services, reportedly grew at average annual rate of 9 percent in 1993–94 through 2001–02.[17] An increasingly affluent population in India has also driven demand for mobile telecommunication services: mobile subscribership increased at a compound annual growth rate of 61 percent from 2004 through 2008.[18] In addition, demand for infrastructure services—particularly energy and transportation—has risen as the government continues to support the growth of both the economy and the middle class in India.[19]

Technological developments have also contributed to rising demand in India's service sector, enabling foreign and domestic companies to outsource business process functions to specialized Indian firms.[20] In the late 1990s, such functions performed by Indian firms primarily comprised call center, data entry, and general administrative and accounting functions. Foreign airline, banking, and computer firms, among others, achieved significant labor cost savings by transferring these operations to Indian service providers.[21] In recent years, the types of outsourced functions performed by Indian firms have become more sophisticated, enabled by the growing expertise of the Indian labor force and the advanced capabilities of IT systems.[22] For instance, Indian firms now provide outsourced functions such as software development, market research, and medical diagnostics. Domestic firms in India, such as those in the finance and telecommunications industries, have also begun to outsource call center and data processing functions, largely to become more competitive in the global marketplace.[23]

Factors Affecting Supply

The supply of services in India has been affected most notably by government deregulation and the rising number of well-educated and highly skilled workers. Government deregulation of certain service industries, such as computer and related services, financial services, and telecommunications, began in the 1990s and, in some cases, included opening these sectors to foreign investment.[24] For instance, the Indian government introduced a National Telecom Policy in 1994, which permitted domestic and foreign private sector participation in India's telecommunications sector. The policy aided the development of India's BPO industry by introducing competition in the provision of basic telecommunications and Internet services.[25] Similarly, the opening of India's computer and financial services industries to foreign direct investment (FDI) has contributed to this growth. Services supply in India has also been facilitated by the increasing education level and skill base of the Indian work force. In 2005, there were an estimated 14 million college graduates in India, many of whom were trained in accounting, finance, and engineering— areas critical to the growth of India's services sector.[26] Nevertheless, there are persistent disparities in quality and access to primary and secondary education, and the demand for high-quality tertiary education exceeds supply.

Services and the Labor Market

Notwithstanding the relative success of the Indian services sector, issues remain—notably, the sector's modest contribution to overall employment growth and the limited size of the highly-skilled workforce. As previously noted, the contribution of the service sector to employment growth in India has been limited, and has been mainly focused in the information technology industry. During the period 1999–2005, employment in India's IT industry increased by more than 250 percent, as compared to only 46 percent in construction services and 27 percent in wholesale and retail services.[27] However, India's IT industry accounted for less than 2 percent of the country's total employment in services in 2005,[28] and employment growth in this industry has been concentrated among high-skilled workers, whereas the vast majority of Indian job seekers are low-skilled.[29] As a result, some observers suggest that sustainable employment growth in India's service sector will have to be achieved in areas that employ a large number of low-skilled workers, such as construction, transportation, and retail distribution services.[30]

While the demand for IT-related services has increased, the supply of IT professionals reportedly has not kept pace with demand. The resulting supply shortage has led to rising wages among IT workers in India, potentially eroding the country's cost advantage in the provision of these services.[31] In response, Indian IT companies have invested in education and worker training programs to offset the skill shortage. Such programs will remain important if the IT industry is to continue to lead growth in the Indian services sector.[32]

INDIA'S INTERNATIONAL TRADE IN SERVICES

The growth in Indian services trade is one of the most significant global trade trends in recent years. Demand for the country's exports led to an Indian services trade surplus of $29.5 billion in 2007, up from $15.4 billion in 2005 (figure 3).[33] Services exports have contributed to economic growth by creating well-paying jobs (both directly in service industries and indirectly through increased consumption by service workers)[34] and by reallocating labor to a high-productivity sector.[35] Services exports have also increased tax revenues and stimulated domestic demand, including demand for electricity, transportation, and communications infrastructure (figure 4).[36]

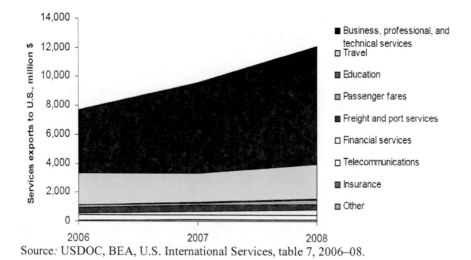

Source: USDOC, BEA, U.S. International Services, table 7, 2006–08.

Figure 3. Business, professional, and technical services were India's top services exports to the U.S. from 2006 through 2008.

The role of service exports in India's economic development is analogous to the role of manufacturing exports in the development of China and other Southeast Asian countries: exporting industries have experienced rapid and sustained growth, creating positive spillover effects in the wider economy. Export growth in both India and China has benefited from the fragmentation of production and the splintering of industries (i.e., firms demanding goods and services from external sources that used to be supplied internally), which has enabled development of complex international supply chains. Production sharing through subcontracting, or through intra-firm sourcing, allows firms to take advantage of the differences in production costs and factor endowments in different markets.[37] Additionally, as the cost of digitizing, transmitting, and processing information has rapidly decreased, cross-border trade has become possible in a growing number of service industries (as an example, one hairdressing shop in Bangalore transmits digital photos of customers' hair to remote hair designers).[38]

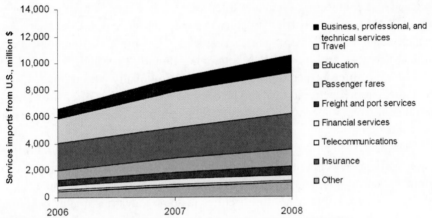

Source: USDOC, BEA, U.S. International Services, table 7, 2006–08.

Figure 4. Travel and education services were India's top services imports from the U.S. from 2006 through 2008.

IT-BPO accounts for the greatest share of India's services exports. As defined by the Government of India Planning Commission, "IT and ITES" (information technology and information technology-enabled services) export revenues grew at an average annual rate of 32 percent from 2001–02 to 2006–07 (from $7.7 billion to $31.3 billion), accounting for 65 percent of the global market in offshore IT by the end of the period.[39] Success in IT-BPO exports has had positive externalities for exports of other knowledge-based services—such as financial services, biotechnology, media, entertainment, and healthcare—which rely on IT infrastructure.[40] It has also provided incentives for math and computer science education; attracted multinational firms which have introduced new skills, technologies, and management techniques to the country; and demonstrated the potential of export-driven growth to other Indian industries.[41]

Among the factors that benefit the competitiveness of Indian services exports is a pool of skilled workers that speak English and have historically received low salaries. In 2010, the estimated salary range for Indian software developers was about \$5,300–\$9,700, compared to \$53,000–\$80,000 in the United States.[42] Public and private educational institutions in India—including the Indian Institutes of Technology, Indian Institute of Science, Indian Institutes of Management, regional public engineering schools, and public-private partnership institutions like Aptech—produce approximately 2.5 million university graduates each year, the second-largest annual number of science and engineering graduates after the United States.[43] Another factor is the lack of regulatory barriers to entry in industries such as software services, which encourages many small start-ups. [44] India's communications infrastructure is still weak but is improving rapidly, benefiting from India's low stock of older-generation technologies. Additionally, specific areas such as Bangalore's Electronic City and Hyderabad's HITEC City offer strong new-generation communications infrastructure, along with office space and social amenities.[45]

Despite these advantages, entrepreneurs in some Indian service industries face barriers. Discretion in license allocation, bureaucratic and regulatory burdens, corruption, and poor infrastructure in many areas raise the costs of doing business. Labor market restrictions in some industries inhibit the hiring and firing of employees. One study by the Organisation for Economic Co-operation and Development (OECD) found that laws governing regular employment contracts in India are stricter than those in Brazil, Chile, China, and all OECD countries except Portugal and the Czech Republic.[46] Further, labor regulations in some states prohibit women from working at night, which can impede efforts to take advantage of time-zone differences. Many domestic firms are suboptimal in size, due in part to India's 1932 Partnership Act, which limited the number of professionals in one firm to 20 (though the 2008 Limited Liability Partnership Act relaxed this restriction). For example, in 2004, only 0.5 percent of accounting firms had more than 10 partners.[47] Laws governing the sale and acquisition of land affect the provision of construction services,[48] and the predominance of government ownership and regulation in the banking sector has led to inefficient lending practices.[49] Inefficiencies in the legal system have made contract enforcement a lengthy process. The World Bank estimates that it took an average of 1,420 days to enforce a contract in India in 2008, as compared to 600 days in Malaysia and 406 days in China, and that the resolution of an insolvency required an average of 10 years in India, as compared to 2 years for both Malaysia and China.[50] These barriers affect both Indian firms and foreign service providers interested in establishing affiliates in India.

In some cases, inadequate enforcement of intellectual property (IP) rights may deter multinational corporations from locating in India,[51] though weak IP protections may have helped India's pharmaceutical and software industries. India's 1970 Patents Act disallows product patents and allows only process patents, a policy that permits reverse engineering (the practice of disassembling technology or ideas to discover their underlying design principles).[52] Multinational corporations have also expressed concern about currency volatility, terrorism, and corporate scandals (such as the recent accounting fraud at Satyam).[53] Barriers vary across states, and generally FDI tends to be concentrated in more business-friendly states such as Andhra Pradesh, Gujarat, Karnataka, Maharashtra, and Tamil Nadu, to the disadvantage of states with more difficult business environments such as Bihar, Uttar Pradesh, and West Bengal.[54] This has led to variation in state GDP growth rates: from 1998 to 2008, the economies of Delhi, Gujarat, and Haryana grew at average annual rates of 7.4 percent, 8.8 percent, and 8.7 percent respectively, while those of Bihar, Madhya Pradesh, and Uttar Pradesh grew at 5.1 percent, 3.5 percent, and 4.4 percent respectively.[55]

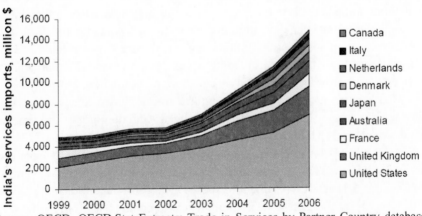

Source: OECD, OECD.Stat Extracts: Trade in Services by Partner Country database (accessed October 1, 2009).

Figure 5. The United States was the top source of India's services imports among OECD countries from 1999 through 2006.

India's services imports have risen significantly in recent years, though less rapidly than its exports. Services imports increased by an average of 17 percent annually from 2005 to 2009, compared to 24 percent for exports.[56] Transportation and business services together accounted for about 50 percent of India's total services imports for the period 2005–09.[57] Among OECD countries, the United States is by far the largest source of India's services imports (figure 5),[58] with education services and travel respectively accounting for 37 and 32 percent of total Indian services imports from the United States from 2001 to 2005.[59]

U.S.-India Services Trade

The United States and India recognize and stress the importance of their relationship in matters both economic and non-economic. Recent milestones in cooperation between the two countries include the approval of the Indo-U.S. civilian nuclear agreement in 2008[60] and adoption of the Framework for Cooperation on Trade and Investment in March 2010.[61]

The United States is the largest export market for Indian services, consuming more of them from 2000 to 2006 than the United Kingdom, France, and Japan—the next-largest importers of Indian services among OECD countries—combined (figure 6).[62] Several factors make the Indian and U.S. economies complementary. English is spoken in India as well as in the United States. Political and legal institutions, as well as accounting practices, are similar in the two countries.[63] The time-zone difference between India and the United States has advantaged IT and other sectors, allowing 24-hour product development and service provision by collaborating teams.

Many Indian nationals have immigrated to the United States to work in service industries. Indian workers accounted for the largest portion of admissions under "H1B" visas in recent years, with 37.8 percent (154,726) of total H1B admissions in 2008.[64] India-based companies were the top sponsors of H1B visas in 2008: Infosys and Wipro received approval for 4,559 and 2,678 visas respectively, while U.S.-based Microsoft received approval for 1,018 visas.[65] Indian software programmers who come to work in the U.S. IT industry experience U.S. standards of service, and many return to India to start new companies with venture capital and expertise acquired in the United States. Indians remaining in the United States serve as a bridging mechanism between the two countries.[66] However, legislation adopted by the United States in August 2010 steeply raised the fees that Indian companies must pay for H1B visas. India lodged immediate and strong objections to the new policy.[67]

By 2001, U.S. companies that had opened software development centers in India included Cisco, Hewlett-Packard, IBM, Lucent, Microsoft, Motorola, Oracle, and Sun Microsystems. NASDAQ's third foreign office is in Bangalore.[68] Some U.S. companies have transitioned from the operation of captive service centers to outsourcing, transferring the ownership of certain IT enterprises in India to domestic investors. Citibank, for example, sold its India-based operations (employing 12,000 people) to Tata Consultancy Services in 2008, with an agreement that the purchasing company would continue to supply Citibank.[69]

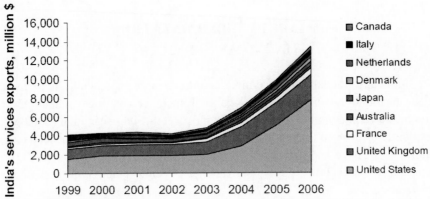

Source: OECD, OECD.Stat Extracts: Trade in Services by Partner Country database (accessed October 1, 2009).

Figure 6. The United States was the top destination for India's services exports among OECD countries from 1999 through 2006.

Meanwhile, Indian firms like Wipro and Infosys have opened offices in the United States, due in part to Indian government efforts to ease restrictions on raising capital abroad and making foreign acquisitions.[70] Since the implementation of these reforms, Indian firms have made increasingly high-value acquisitions in the United States, such as the acquisition by VSNL (now Tata Communications Limited) of U.S. firm Teleglobe International Holdings for $254 million in 2005.[71]

The history of U.S. firms establishing affiliates in India has been marked by some reversals. In 1951, IBM was invited to establish an accounting machine plant in Mumbai, but left India in 1977 due to government pressure to allow partial Indian ownership of local manufacturing, sales, and maintenance operations. This departure was a factor in the growth of Tata Consultancy Services, which partially filled the vacuum left by IBM in supplying high-value services to multinational firms.[72]

Outsourcing is increasingly motivated by careful assessments of value chains and competitive advantages,[73] and some U.S. companies have recently reversed their outsourcing efforts altogether. In 2009, for example, Delta Airlines closed its call centers in India and relocated those functions to the United States in an attempt to improve customer service, and Dell offers a premium technical support option which guarantees that American customers will be able to speak with U.S.-based customer service representatives.[74]

MARKET LIBERALIZATION IN INDIAN SERVICES

India has gradually become more ambitious in its approach to multilateral trade negotiations, as its potential gains from other countries' reductions in import barriers continue to increase. India's Tenth Five Year Plan (2002–07) explicitly prioritized international negotiations, arguing that India needed to be more "aggressive and proactive" in the World Trade Organization (WTO).[75] Further, India's 2004–2009 First National Foreign Trade Policy explicitly recognized the country's potential to become a hub for export-oriented services, and established the Services Export Promotion Council to look for specific export opportunities.[76] India still has strong domestic constituencies promoting traditional goals of economic self-sufficiency and protection for its agricultural sectors but, over time, services exporters have gained political salience.

India has scheduled commitments under the General Agreement on Trade in Services (GATS) in business services, communications, construction, financial services, health services, and tourism.[77] India's revised Doha Round offer (a 2005 update of its initial offer) proposed new commitments or improvements to existing commitments in a number of industries, including but not limited to air transport, architectural services, computer services, construction, distribution, education, financial services, telecommunications, and tourism.[78] Due to autonomous liberalization undertaken since the Uruguay Round, India could make significant Doha Round commitments to bind de facto liberalization levels without encountering economic disruption. In exchange for binding actual levels of openness, India hopes to gain services concessions as well as reductions in agricultural subsidies in developed countries[79] and increased flexibility on compulsory license issues related to the Agreement on Trade-Related Aspects of Intellectual Property Rights (TRIPS).[80] However, the Office of the U.S. Trade Representative (USTR) contends that India's revised offer would provide only minor and incremental improvements that are insufficiently responsive to members' demands.[81]

India's priorities in trade negotiations include securing access to foreign markets via cross-border trade (mode 1)[82] and the presence of natural persons (mode 4),[83] the primary modes of delivery for services such as R&D and engineering. Mode 4 liberalization is an especially high priority given the high number of Indian services professionals prepared to offer services abroad and the significant restrictions in many developed countries' immigration policies.[84] Among its requests of developed countries, India has requested that the United States remove quotas on the entry of professionals, eliminate state-by-state licensing for foreign service providers, and remove the stipulation requiring market entrants in specialty occupations to possess highly specialized knowledge.[85] India can also achieve some gains from other countries' liberalization of impediments to the provision of services through consumption abroad (mode 2),[86] such as restrictions on the cross-border portability of health insurance (the cost of coronary bypass surgery in India is as little as 5 percent of the cost in developed countries).[87]

India has been active in forming bilateral and regional trade agreements, including free trade agreements (FTAs) with Sri Lanka and Singapore, and the South Asian Free Trade Area (SAFTA). The India-Singapore agreement eliminates limits on the number of service suppliers and on the total value of service transactions between the countries. It also gives Singapore preferential treatment in the provision of construction, financial services, telecommunication services, and tourism, while India receives preferential treatment in the provision of distribution, education, and environmental services. In addition, both countries offer preferential treatment in the provision of each other's transport and business services.[88] India and Sri Lanka are building on their 1998 FTA by negotiating an additional Comprehensive Economic Partnership Agreement that will add commitments on services,[89] and SAFTA signatories are currently negotiating the inclusion of trade in services in that agreement.[90] India is also currently working with ASEAN countries to liberalize trade in services, and has requested that ASEAN countries open their markets to Indian exports of accounting, architecture, education, and healthcare services.[91] India is part of the Asia-Pacific Trade

Agreement (APTA)[92] and the Global System of Trade Preferences among Developing Countries,[93] and has established preferential trade agreements (PTAs) with Afghanistan, Chile, Thailand, and Mercosur. On the other hand, the 2005 India-EU Strategic Partnership Joint Action Plan agrees only to initiate strategic sectoral dialogues on services-related regulatory policy (including mutual recognition agreements, domestic regulation, and market access issues), and the 2005 India-U.S. Trade Policy Forum Joint Statement is limited to the establishment of focus groups on barriers to trade in services.[94]

India has geopolitical motivations for increasing economic cooperation in South Asia,[95] though concerns regarding the balance between access for services exporters and domestic protectionist interests apply to the pursuit of services liberalization under regional trade agreements just as they do to WTO liberalization.[96] In particular, India's strategic perspective is shaped by the challenges and opportunities presented by China's economic and military influence in Asia. India and China have expressed interest in trade agreements with each other, and a joint task force studying the feasibility of such agreements has recently released a draft report covering services trade.[97]

India has implemented substantial autonomous liberalization and privatization reforms. After India's 1991 balance of payments crisis, the country phased out import restrictions, reduced tariffs, opened service industries to FDI (including banking, insurance, telecommunications, transport, health and education, and broadcasting), and encouraged the entry of multinational corporations by establishing export processing zones and special economic zones.[98] Software Technology Parks—special zones designated for export-oriented activities—were established in the 1990s, providing firms with high-quality infrastructure, tax holidays until 2010, duty-free equipment imports, and permission for up to 100 percent FDI. By July 2004, there were 40 parks set up under the scheme, including ones in Bangalore and Hyderabad.[99] India's industrial policy reforms include abolishing the requirement that investments by large firms go through a time-consuming, separate clearance process under the Monopolies and Restrictive Trade Practices Act; India replaced that law with a new law regulating anticompetitive practices in 2002.[100]

In the initial years after the 1991 crisis, the Indian government pursued disinvestment—the sale of minority stakes in public sector firms—with hopes of raising revenue and improving the performance of the firms. Disinvestment raised less revenue than policymakers had hoped because investors did not wish to purchase shares of firms that would remain under government management. In 1998, the government announced a transition from disinvestment to privatization, in which it would reduce its holdings in many public sector firms to 26 percent. The subsequent year saw the first privatization of a public sector firm when 74 percent of the equity in Modern Foods India Ltd (a bakery with 2,000 employees) was sold to an Indian subsidiary of Unilever.[101]

India also has liberalized its laws on overseas investment by Indian firms. Starting in 2000, Indian companies were allowed to invest 100 percent of the proceeds from issuing shares (a common method of financing outward FDI) to acquire foreign companies.[102] Among other liberalization efforts, in 2002, the limit on Indian investment in foreign joint ventures and wholly-owned subsidiaries was increased from $50 million to $100 million per financial year; in 2004, Indian firms were allowed to borrow in foreign exchange for direct investments in foreign joint ventures and subsidiaries; in 2007, the limit on overseas investment by Indian companies was raised to 400 percent of the investing firm's net worth; and in 2008, the limit on overseas investment by India-based mutual funds was increased to $7 billion.[103]

At present, significantly liberalized Indian service industries include computer services and telecoms. Moderately liberalized sectors include financial services, construction, health, and air transport. Accountancy, legal services, and distribution remain highly restricted.[104]

As a democracy, India provides representation to groups both supportive and skeptical of liberalization. In one example of the latter, the Communist Party of India prevented a parliamentary vote on a set of financial reforms, including a bill raising the limits on foreign ownership of Indian insurance firms, during the 14th Lok Sabha (lower house of Parliament) from 2005 to 2009.[105] Concern for displaced workers has slowed liberalization in low-skilled, labor intensive service industries such as construction. In protected industries that employ highly-skilled workers, such as legal services, impediments to liberalization are maintained due to the political influence of current beneficiaries.[106]

POTENTIAL EFFECTS
OF ADDITIONAL LIBERALIZATION

We use gravity models to evaluate the potential effects of further liberalization on India's cross-border imports of services. Gravity models examine the relationship between certain variables—such as economic size, distance, and other potential sources of "trade resistance"[107]—and the volume of trade between two countries. Tinbergen developed the basic gravity model nearly 50 years ago,[108] and an extensive literature of gravity model-based studies has emerged in the decades since. While gravity models have been used to analyze trade in goods more often than trade in services, studies such as those by Grünfeld and Moxnes[109] and by Kimura and Lee[110] have demonstrated their usefulness for analysis of services trade.

The starting point for our models is the "standard"[111] gravity equation:

$$lnIM_{ij} = \beta_1 + \beta_2\ lnY_i + \beta_3\ lnY_j + \beta_4 ln\ D_{ij} + \varepsilon_{ij}$$

where $_{IMij}$ is country i's imports from country j; Yi and Yj are the gross domestic product (GDP) of countries i and j, respectively;[112] $_{Dij}$ is the distance from country i to country j; and $_{\varepsilon ij}$ is the error term. The log-log specification makes it easier to analyze the elasticity of trade volumes with respect to the trading partners' GDP and the distance between them.

Gravity studies have sought to account for a variety of additional factors influencing the volume of trade. Following Kimura and Lee, we include dummy variables for adjacency and common language.[113] The adjacency variable traditionally controls for country pairs that share a border; we extend this to include country pairs located across a small sea. The intuition is that direct neighbors should trade more because they face lower transaction costs. The common language variable captures the idea that countries that share a language—and the broader cultural affinities associated with the use of that language—may face lower costs to trade.

Nontariff measures (NTMs) may also affect flows of trade in services (unlike goods, tariffs are not applied to services). Grünfeld and Moxnes, Kimura and Lee, and Walsh[114] use a variety of measures in their models in order to capture the effects of NTMs on services trade.[115] We use a new measure: an index of restrictions on inward FDI in services developed by Golub.[116]

FDI restrictiveness scores are useful proxies for barriers to cross-border trade in services because FDI facilitates services trade, while restrictions on FDI inhibit trade.[117] A number of studies explore this relationship. Fillat-Castejón, Francois, and Wörz examine the extent to which FDI inflows and cross-border imports of services are complements or substitutes. They find strong evidence of FDI's complementary effect on services imports, in both the short and the long run. Furthermore, they find that barriers to foreign ownership have a significant, negative effect on cross-border imports of services.[118] These findings buttress those of Grünfeld and Moxnes, who create gravity models that use service exports and the stock of outward FDI in services as dependent variables. They test for complementarity by regressing the residuals from the FDI model on the residuals from the exports model, and find a positive and highly significant relationship, meaning that services exports and investment move in tandem.[119]

Golub's index has a number of advantages over other measures of restrictiveness: it is specific to services; it measures "applied" barriers (as opposed to those "bound" in WTO commitments); and it covers more countries (73) and industries (eight) than other measures of applied services NTMs. Golub scores the countries on a scale of 0 (least restrictive) to 1 (most restrictive), accounting for regulations on foreign ownership, screening and approval, as well as operational restrictions for the period 2004–05 (table 2).

Table 2. FDI restriction scoring method

Foreign Ownership	
No foreign equity allowed	1
1–19% foreign equity allowed	0.6
20–34% foreign equity allowed	0.5
35–49% foreign equity allowed	0.4
50–74% foreign equity allowed	0.2
75–99% foreign equity allowed	0.1
Screening and approval	
Investor must show economic benefits	0.2
Approval unless contrary to national interest	0.1
Notification (pre- or post-establishment)	0.05
Operational Restrictions	
Board of directors/managers	
majority must be nationals or residents	0.1
at least one must be national or resident	0.05
Duration of work permit for expatriates	
less than one year	0.1
one to two years	0.05
three to four years	0.025
Other operational restrictions	up to 0.1
Total (capped at 1.0)	*Between 0 and 1*

Source: Golub, "Openness to Foreign Direct Investment in Services," 2009.

He assesses barriers in eight industries: business services, telecommunications, construction, distribution, electricity, financial services, tourism, and travel. Golub uses an average of FDI and trade weights to generate an index score for overall restrictions on services FDI for each country.

Our model also includes a remoteness variable to control for the effects of "relative distance": countries that are close to each other but far from the rest of the world can be expected to trade more with each other than the rest of the world. We define remoteness (REM) as

$$REM_i = \Sigma d_{im}/y_m$$

where d_{im} is the distance from country i to all trade partners, and y_m is the GDP of the trading partners of country i.[120]

We estimate our model two ways: first, with random effects[121] with year dummies from 2000 to 2006, and secondly, with ordinary least squares (OLS) for 2004:

1. $lnIM_{jit} = \beta_1 + \beta_2\, lnY_{it} + \beta_3\, lnY_{jt} + \beta_4\, lnD_{ij} + \beta_5\, A_{ij} + \beta_6\, CL_{ij} + \beta_7\, SFDIR_i + \beta_8 lnREM_{it} + \beta_9 lnREM_{jt} + \beta_{10}Y01 + \beta_{11}Y02 + \beta_{12}Y03 + \beta_{13}Y04 + \beta_{14}Y05 + \beta_{15}Y06 + \varepsilon_{ij}$

2. $lnIM_{ji} = \beta_1 + \beta_2\, lnY_i + \beta_3\, lnY_j + \beta_4\, lnD_{ij} + \beta_5\, A_{ij} + \beta_6\, CL_{ij} + \beta_7\, SFDIR_i + \beta_8 lnREM_i + \beta_9 lnREM_j + \varepsilon_{ij}$

where A_{ij} and CL_{ij} are adjacency and common language dummies; $SFDIRi$ is the overall services FDI restrictiveness index for the importing country i; $REMit$ and $REMjt$ are the remoteness of countries i and j, respectively, in period t; and $Y01$–$Y06$ are year dummies in the random effects model.[122] We use 2004 data for the OLS model because it is one of the two years for which the $SFDIR$ data were collected. The bilateral service imports data are taken from OECD's Statistics on International Trade in Services, which contains 26 OECD countries and Russia as exporters, along with 70 importing countries.[123] The World Bank's World Development Indicators (WDI) is the source for GDP, measured in 2000 constant U.S. dollars. Distance, adjacency, and common language are calculated by the Centre d'Etudes Prospectives et d'Informations Internationales.

Table 3. Gravity model: Dependent variable— ln(Services Imports)

	Random effects	OLS
Services FDI restrictiveness	-1.373 ‡	-1.314 ‡
	(-3.85)	(-3.41)
ln (importer's GDP)	0.914 ‡	0.850 ‡
	(29.62)	(25.73)
ln (exporter's GDP)	1.809 ‡	0.987 ‡
	(16.64)	(25.51)
ln (distance)	-1.214 ‡	-0.996 ‡
	(-16.9)	(-12.44)
ln (importer's remoteness)	0.186†	0.012
	(2.03)	(0.12)
ln (exporter's remoteness)	0.746 ‡	0.121
	(6.94)	(1.43)
Adjacency	0.096	0.272
	(0.61)	(1.26)
Common language	1.177 ‡	1.163 ‡
	(7.3)	(6.84)
Constant	-45.664 ‡	-33.396 ‡
	(-19.66)	(-14.46)
Year01	-0.008	
	(-0.25)	
Year02	0.037	
	(1.25)	
Year03	0.238 ‡	
	(7.84)	
Year04	0.451 ‡	
	(14.57)	
Year05	0.509 ‡	
	(15.67)	
Year06	0.349 ‡	
	(4.56)	
Number of observations	4455	858
Overall/adjusted r-squared	0.737	0.700

‡ significant at the 1 percent level.
† significant at the 5 percent level.

Results

The services FDI restrictiveness index is right skewed, meaning that most countries in the dataset are relatively open. The most restrictive score is only 67 percent of the maximum possible. The 2004 data are very similar overall to the panel data. The variables are highly correlated in a few instances, but not so broadly as to undermine the model (appendix tables A.1–A.4).

In both specifications, GDP is strongly and positively associated with exports, while distance is strongly and negatively associated with trade, as expected. Remoteness has a positive effect in the panel regression, with increased significance over the OLS model. Adjacency has a slightly positive but insignificant effect.

This may be due to the fact that there are very few country pairs in the dataset that are adjacent; it could also suggest that sharing a border is less important for trade in services than trade in goods. The common language variable has a highly positive and significant effect on trade. The adjusted R-squared values for the random effects and OLS model are .737 and .700, respectively, meaning that the model explains about 70 percent of the variation in cross-border imports of services (table 3).

The services FDI restrictiveness index has a highly significant explanatory effect in both models, although the effect and its level of significance are slightly greater in the random effects model. The results suggest that a decrease of 0.01 in a country's restrictiveness score is associated with about a 1.3 percent increase in imports of services into that country.

Potential Effects of Future Liberalization in India

India's services FDI restrictiveness index score is 0.38. Using the random effects model, we can examine the possible effects of further FDI liberalization for India. If India were to reduce FDI restrictions to the mean index score (0.24), cross-border imports into India could be expected to increase by approximately 19.2 percent, ceteris paribus. If India liberalized to the minimum index score (0.04), cross-border imports into India could be expected to increase by approximately 46.7 percent.

Table 4. Potential effects of further liberalization

| | Services imports, 2005, actual ($ billion) | Increase in imports (percent) | Liberalization to mean level of restrictiveness measured by Golub | | Liberalization to minimum level of restrictiveness measured by Golub |
			Services imports, 2005, with further liberalization ($ billion)	Increase in imports (percent)	Services imports, 2005, with further liberalization ($ billion)
Random effects	$14.4	19.2	$17.2	46.7	$21.1
OLS	$14.4	18.4	$17.0	44.7	$20.8

In 2005, India imported approximately $14.4 billion of services from 24 countries in the model.[124] Liberalizing to the mean score on the services FDI restrictiveness index would increase imports to approximately $17.2 billion, and liberalization to the minimum score would increase imports to $21.1 billion (table 4).

PART II: SERVICE INDUSTRY PROFILES

Information Technology and Business Process Outsourcing (IT-BPO) Services

Overview

Over the past decade, IT-BPO services (box 1) have emerged as key contributors to India's export earnings, investment, employment, and overall economic and social development.[125] Competitive labor costs, English language skills, technical expertise, political stability, favorable tax rates, and a reputation for high-quality services have driven the sector's rapid growth.[126] IT-BPO revenue in India totaled $64.1 billion in FY 2008.[127] Its share of GDP grew from 1.2 percent in fiscal year[128] (FY) 1998 to an estimated 5.5 percent in FY 2008, with the industry growing at an average annual rate of about 31 percent from FY 2004 to FY 2008.[129] The industry employed approximately two million people within India in FY 2008, an increase of about 24 percent over FY 2007.[130]

Box 1. Defining the IT-BPO Industry

It is difficult to generate consistent statistics for IT-BPO services because they do not fit neatly within common industrial classification systems. From one source to another, definitions of the industry often span similar but not identical lists of activities. For example, the International Monetary Fund defines computer and information services as "resident/nonresident transactions related to hardware consultancy, software implementation, information services (data processing, database, news agency), and maintenance and repair of computers and related equipment."[a] By comparison, the Bureau of Economic Analysis (BEA) of the U.S.

Department of Commerce (USDOC) defines computer and data processing services as "data entry processing (both batch and remote), and tabulation; computer systems analysis, design, and engineering; custom software and programming services (including Web design); integrated hardware/software systems; and other computer services (timesharing, maintenance, Web site management, and repair)."[b] The BEA notes that computer-related services may be embedded in goods that are exported to foreign markets and that the total value of computer services trade may be scattered across several categories.[c] IT-enabled services also often contain characteristics of audiovisual and telecommunication services, as well as specialized professional services such as engineering and accountancy. [d]

In the interest of consistency, we employ the definition of IT-BPO used by the National Association of Software and Service Companies (NASSCOM), India's most prominent association for the IT-BPO industry, unless indicated otherwise. It includes IT outsourcing (information systems outsourcing, network and desktop outsourcing, application management, hosted application management, and hosted infrastructure services); project-based services (IT consulting, systems integration, network consulting and integration, custom application development); support and training (hardware deployment and support, software deployment and support, IT education and training); and BPO (customer management, finance and accounting, human resource administration, training, and procurement).[e]

a IMF, "Balance of Payments Statistics," September 4, 2007.
b USDOC, BEA, "Quarterly Survey of Transactions," January 2010, 16.
c USDOC, BEA, *Survey of Currency Business*, October 2008, 25.
d USITC, "Computer and Related Services," June 2007, 5-1 to 5-2.
e NASSCOM, *Strategic Review 2009*, February 2009, 25, 30.

The seven largest IT-BPO firms accounted for nearly 50 percent of the industry's export revenues in FY 2008 and nearly 35 percent of employment. Yet most firms in the industry are small: nearly 90 percent of firms have annual revenues of less than $10 million while accounting for about 17 percent of the industry's labor force.[131] The leading IT services firms during FY 2009 were Tata Consultancy Services (TCS), Wipro, Infosys, Hewlett-Packard India, and IBM India (table 5), while the top BPO firms were Genpact, TCS BPO, WNS Global Services, Wipro BPO, and Firstsource Solutions (table 6).[132]

Table 5. Top information technology firms in India, FY 2009

Rank	Company	Country of corporate parent	FY 2008 revenues (rupees crore)[a]	FY 2008 revenues ($ million)[b]	FY 2009 revenues (rupees crore)	FY 2009 revenues ($ million)[c]	Percent change, FY 2008 to FY 2009 (rupees)
1	Tata Consultancy Services (TCS)	India	21,215	5,266	25,894	5,572	22
2	Wipro	India	16,884	4,191	23,882	5,139	41
3	Infosys Technologies	India	15,531	3,855	20,392	4,388	31
4	Hewlett-Packard India	United States	15,454	3,836	15,763	3,392	2
5	IBM India	United States	10,101	2,507	12,048	2,593	19
6	Cognizant Technology	United States	6,310	1,566	9,410	2,025	49
7	Ingram Micro[d]	United States	8,620	2,140	9,396	2,022	9
8	HCL Technologies	India	6,200	1,539	8,764	1,886	41
9	HCL Infosystems[d]	India	5,058	1,256	8,089	1,741	60
10	Redington India[d]	India	6,280	1,559	6,576	1,415	5

Sources: Dataquest, DQ Top20 2009, July 11, 2009; Bureau van Dijk, Orbis database (accessed June 25, 2010).

[a] 1 crore equals 10 million rupees.

[b] Rupees converted to dollars using average rates for interbank exchange for April 1, 2007 through March 31, 2008 ($1 = Rs. 40.29). Oanda, Historical Exchange Rates database.

[c] Rupees converted to dollars using average rates for interbank exchange for April 1, 2008 through March 31, 2009 ($1 = Rs. 46.47). Oanda, Historical Exchange Rates database.

[d] Company whose primary business is hardware manufacturing and/or distribution.

Table 6. Top business process outsourcing firms in India , FY 2009

Rank	Company	Country of corporate parent	FY 2008 revenues (rupees crore)[a]	FY 2008 revenues ($ million)[b]	FY 2009 revenues (rupees crore)	FY 2009 revenues ($ million)[c]	Percent change, FY2008 to FY2009 (rupees)
1	Genpact	India	2,659	660	4,086	879	54
2	TCS BPO	India	1,386	344	1,817	391	31
3	WNS Global	India[d]	1,171	291	1,781	383	52
4	Wipro BPO	India	1,147	285	1,641	353	43
5	Firstource Solutions	India	1,164	289	1,560	336	34
6	Aegis BPO	India	851	211	1,558	335	83
7	IBM Daksh	United States	1,292	321	1,486	320	15
8	Infosys BPO	India	977	243	1,471	317	51
9	Aditya Birla Minacs	India	1,563	388	1,430	308	−9
10	HCL BPO	India	880	218	1,077	232	22

Source: Dataquest, The DQ BPO Top20, July 25, 2009; Bureau van Dijk, Orbis database (accessed June 25, 2010); company Web sites.

[a] 1 crore equals 10 million rupees.

[b] Rupees converted to dollars using average rates for interbank exchange for April 1, 2007 through March 31, 2008 ($1 = Rs. 40.29). Oanda, Historical Exchange Rates database.

[c] Rupees converted to dollars using average rates for interbank exchange for April 1, 2008 through March 31, 2009 ($1 = Rs. 46.47). Oanda, Historical Exchange Rates database.

[d] Incorporated in Jersey, Channel Islands; headquartered in India.

Participation in Global Trade

India's IT-BPO exports totaled approximately $40.4 billion in FY 2008, accounting for about 63 percent of the industry's total revenue.[133] While low-end services such as software installation and support and offshore call center operations historically have been key Indian IT-BPO exports, Indian companies have been expanding into higher valued-added services. Segments such as infrastructure management services, package implementation, testing, and consulting have experienced rapid growth over the last few years. The increased provision of these high-value service lines is enabling Indian companies to expand sales to existing customers, charge higher average billing rates for new contracts, and increase their recognition as providers of both basic and high-end IT-BPO services.[134]

The United States and the United Kingdom are the top export markets for Indian IT-BPO services, respectively accounting for 60 percent ($24.2 billion) and 19 percent ($7.7 billion) of the industry's export revenues in FY 2008. Continental Europe[135] also has been emerging as an important market for the Indian IT-BPO industry, as exports to the region increased at an average annual rate of over 50 percent from FY 2004 through FY 2008. [136] Banking, financial services, and insurance (BFSI) high-tech, and telecommunications companies remain the leading customers for Indian IT-BPO firms; together, they accounted for about 61 percent of Indian IT-BPO services revenues in FY 2008. Retail, health care, and utility firms are also becoming increasingly important consumers of Indian IT-BPO services.[137]

Domestic and Cross-border Investment

India allows 100 percent FDI in IT-BPO.[138] The country's latest offer in the WTO's Doha Round negotiations includes a binding commitment to maintain this policy.[139] FDI inflows in IT-BPO totaled approximately $1.0 billion in FY 2008, an increase of 25 percent from 2007.[140] U.S. firms, including some of the largest IT-BPO service providers in the world,[141] have been very active in the Indian market.

For example, IBM opened a cloud computing[142] center in Bangalore in September 2008 to serve Indian businesses and public institutions.[143]

The industry has witnessed a rise in merger and acquisition (M&A) activity in recent years as companies have sought to establish a presence in their clients' home markets, to gain new clients, and to hire local talent in developing markets.[144] The number of deals declined from 159 in 2007 to 98 in 2008 while the value increased from $2.9 billion to $3.4 billion, indicating a higher average deal size. Major M&A deals completed in 2008 included the acquisition by HCL Technologies of UK consulting firm Axon for about $658 million, TCS' purchase of Citi's BPO arm for $505 million, and Wipro's acquisition of Citi Technology Services for $127 million.[145]

Indian IT-BPO service providers have rapidly expanded their operations outside India. An "indicative list" of locations where Indian IT-BPO firms have service delivery centers, published in 2009, listed 61 countries on every continent except Antarctica.[146] Firms have several motivations for establishing operations outside India. In established markets such as North America and

Europe (as well as new markets in Asia and elsewhere), local offices enable firms to offer in-person services (e.g., management consulting) in combination with those delivered at a distance. Service centers in Latin America, Eastern Europe, and Africa offer the firms access to workers who speak a broader array of languages, and whose cultural ties with client markets may enhance customer satisfaction.[147] Operations in other countries also help Indian firms hedge against the risk of rupee appreciation vis-à-vis the dollar, which decreases competitiveness.[148]

Factors Affecting Demand

Factors affecting demand for India's IT-BPO services include economic and financial conditions in key export markets, the relative attractiveness of competing providers, and changes in the domestic market for outsourced IT-BPO services.

The global financial crisis and subsequent economic downturn significantly affected large ITBPO companies in India, as they derive much of their business from BFSI firms based in the United States and Western Europe—among the hardest-hit industries and regions during the downturn.[149] However, demand for Indian IT-BPO exports rebounded in the second half of 2009, with the United States and developing markets in the Asia Pacific serving as engines of renewed demand.[150] Satyam, one of the top Indian IT-BPO firms, lost important customers in the wake of an accounting scandal in January 2009,[151] but the overall impact of the scandal on the Indian IT-BPO industry appears to have been modest.[152]

Competition from other countries also affects demand for India's IT-BPO services. Factors that affect attractiveness for outsourcing include the costs of labor, infrastructure services, and regulatory compliance (including taxes); the size, skills, and language abilities of the labor force; and the broader business environment, including the quality of infrastructure and protection of intellectual property. Since 2004, consulting firm A.T. Kearney's Global Services Location Index (GSLI) has ranked countries' attractiveness based on these factors, and India has topped the index every year. Some countries score higher than India on specific elements of the GSLI—for example, Ghana, Indonesia, Vietnam, and the Philippines were all judged more "financially attractive" (i.e., cheaper) in 2009. But no country offers the same combination of a skilled labor market and relatively welcoming business environment at such low costs. A.T. Kearney predicts that India will retain its lead over its competitors "for the foreseeable future," despite cost pressures (see below), the Satyam scandal, and concerns about terrorism after the Mumbai attacks of November 2008.[153]

Indian firms' demand for outsourced IT-BPO services has grown as they have sought to increase service quality and efficiency.[154] IT-BPO service providers, in turn, have increased their focus on attracting these potential domestic clients. Industries in which demand has been strong include telecommunications, retail, logistics and transportation, BFSI, and manufacturing, as well as the Indian government.[155] In contrast to clients from developed countries, Indian firms do not outsource to take advantage of wage differentials, as there is little difference between the pay offered by the IT-BPO providers and client companies. Instead, clients value the specialized skills that the IT-BPO firms can offer.[156] Contracts have grown increasingly large and complex. For example, in 2008, the telecommunications company Aircel awarded a nine-year, $500 million contract to Wipro to design, implement, and operate a comprehensive IT platform for delivery of cutting-edge telecommunications services.[157]

Factors Affecting Supply

Workforce challenges and government incentives affect the industry's supply of services. Among the former, attrition, wage inflation, and skill levels pose particular challenges. High attrition tends to undermine the quality of services and to boost costs for recruitment and training.[158] And attrition is a problem for India: a 2007 study found that nearly 60 percent of call center employees in India had less than one year of tenure, compared to less than 30 percent in the United Kingdom, United States, and Canada.[159] In order to reduce attrition, firms have raised wages: pay in the IT-BPO sector was increasing by 10–15 percent per year before the downturn.[160] The decrease in demand for IT-BPO services associated with the economic slowdown appeared to temper both attrition and wage inflation,[161] although they are expected to increase again as the economies of key export markets recover.[162]

IT-BPO companies also face a shortage of qualified talent—the industry's core asset. According to NASSCOM, the industry could face a deficit of up to 3.5 million workers over the next decade due to the low employability of Indian graduates.[163] A 2005 report estimated that only about 25 percent of technical graduates and 10–15 percent of general graduates from Indian colleges and universities were suited for employment in the IT-BPO sector.[164]

In response, NASSCOM has initiated programs such as the NASSCOM Assessment Certificate (NAC) and National Faculty Development Program (NFDP) to provide additional training and improve IT education standards at Indian schools.[165]

Finally, government incentives for IT-related industries have supported the sector's development. The Software Technology Parks of India program (STPI), created in 1991, exempts eligible firms from taxes on export profits, customs and excise duties, and service and sales taxes. Unlike India's Special Economic Zones (SEZs), the STPI does not require firms to be based in a particular location to be eligible for benefits.[166] The STPI program is scheduled to end in March 2011. Some small IT-BPO firms are concerned that the ending of the STPI program could disadvantage them vis-à-vis larger firms, as moving to the SEZs in order to remain eligible for benefits could prove prohibitively expensive.[167]

TELECOMMUNICATION SERVICES

Overview

Sweeping liberalization and deregulation undertaken by successive governments over the past decade have transformed the Indian telecommunication services industry from a market dominated by a few government-controlled entities into one characterized by a large number of private sector rivals and high levels of competition. Such competition has resulted in declining service prices, which have, in turn, led to rapid market growth.[168] From 2004 through 2008, for example, the total number of telephone subscribers grew at a compound annual growth rate (CAGR) of 43 percent to approximately 385 million, causing total telephone subscriber penetration[169] to increase from 9 percent to 33 percent (table 7). By the end of 2009, the number of telephone subscribers in India had grown to 562 million, pushing total penetration to 45 percent. This growth was driven almost entirely by the mobile telephone segment, which accounted for approximately 93 percent of India's total telephone connections in 2009, up from approximately 52 percent in 2004.[170]

Table 7. India: Telecommunication services market statistics, 2004–08

	2004	2005	2006	2007	2008	1-year change, 2007 to 2008 (%)	CAGR,[a] 2004-07 (%)
Telecommunication services revenues (US$ million)	14,389	16,660	18,387	21,145	24,317	15	14
Total telephone subscribers	92,760	124,780	189,920	272,874	384,804	41	43
Total telephone penetration[b]	8.6	11.4	17.2	23.9	33.2		
Fixed telephone lines ('000)	40,860	41,040	40,300	39,254	37,914	−3.4	90 2c
Fixed-line penetration (%)	3.8	3.8	3.6	3.4	3.3		
Fixed-line growth (%)	−3.0	0.4	−1.8	−2.6	−3.4		
Mobile subscribers ('000)	51,900	83,740	149,620	233,620	346,890	49	65
Mobile penetration (%)	4.8	7.7	13.5	20.4	30.0		
Mobile growth (%)	82.8	61.3	78.7	56.1	48.5		
Mobile share of total telephone subscribers (%)	56	67	79	86	90		
Internet Subscribers ('000)	5,450	6,800	8,582	10,360	12,850	24	24
Internet Users ('000)	35,000	60,000	75,522	88,060	107,940	23	36
Internet Penetration (%)	0.5	0.6	0.8	0.9	1.1		
Internet Growth (%)	32	25	26	21	24		

Source: Hot Telecom, Country Profile: India, July 2009.

Regulatory Environment

In India, the telecommunication services market is administered by the Ministry of Communications and Information Technology (MoC), which is divided into two main divisions: the Department of Telecommunications (DoT) and the Department of Information Technology.[171] The DoT is the main governing body in India's telecommunication services market, with key responsibilities including formulating policy, granting licenses, administering laws, cooperating with international telecommunication bodies, and promoting standardization and research and development (R&D). It also administers the Telecom Commission,[172] the Telecom Regulatory Authority of India (TRAI) (see below), and the Telecom Disputes Settlement and Appellate Tribunal.[173] Finally, the DoT is responsible for managing Bharat Sanchar Nigam Limited (BSNL) and Mahanagar Telephone Nigam Limited (MTNL), in which the government controls equity shares of 100 percent and 56 percent, respectively.[174]

In 1997, the government created the semiautonomous TRAI to regulate the Indian telecommunications sector.[175] Broadly, the TRAI is responsible for monitoring service quality, protecting consumer interests, resolving disputes between operators, approving certain service tariffs,[176] establishing interconnection terms and conditions, and ensuring compliance with licensing conditions, among other functions.[177]

The Indian Telegraph Act establishes the basic legal framework of the Indian telecommunication services market. Enacted in 1885, the act gives the government of India the power to, inter alia, grant licenses, regulate tariff prices, establish rules of conduct, arbitrate disputes, and install and maintain telephone lines.[178] Other important legislation pertaining to the Indian telecommunication services market includes the Indian Wireless Act, 1933; the Telecom Regulatory Authority of India Act, 1997; the Telecom Regulatory Authority (Amendment) Ordinance, 2000; the Communications Convergence Bill, 2001; and the Broadband Policy, 2004.[179]

Although the Indian Telegraph Act laid out the structure of the telecommunication services market, the National Telecom Policy 1994 established objectives and targets for the industry.[180] In response to rapid technological changes, the New Telecom Policy was issued in 1999 (NTP-99). In addition to setting new industry objectives/targets and clarifying issues pertaining to spectrum management, universal service obligations, and the role of the TRAI, the NTP-99 encouraged competition by allowing operators in the fixed-line, wireless, Internet, satellite, and cable television sectors to enter one another's markets.[181]

For licensing and administrative purposes, India is divided into 22 telecommunication service areas, referred to as "circles." The DoT issues four types of licenses for the provision of telecommunications service within these circles: the basic service operator (BSO) license, the cellular mobile telecommunication services (CMTS) license, the Universal Access Services (UAS) license, and the Internet Service Provider (ISP) license. Although licenses are issued to carriers for operations in a specific circle, applicants are typically allowed to apply for licenses in multiple circles. BSO and CMTS licenses, which date to the 1990s, allow holders to offer fixed-line and wireless services, respectively. By contrast, the UAS license, which was introduced in 2003, allows holders to offer fixed, wireless, and data services.[182]

In January 2008, facing a large backlog of UAS license applications, the DoT announced that such licenses would be issued to all applicants. However, in August 2009, the TRAI asked the DoT to stop issuing new licenses, citing the lack of frequency spectrum necessary to accommodate all applicants. By the end of March 2010, 241 UAS licenses had been issued by the DoT. [183] India's domestic long-distance (DLD) and international long-distance (ILD) markets were liberalized in 2000 and 2002, respectively. In 2006, to further increase competition in DLD/ILD markets, the TRAI substantially reduced licensing fees and authorized non-telecommunication companies with fiber optic networks to enter the market. By April 2010, 29 DLD providers had been licensed, with five operators having launched services, as well as 13 privately owned ILD operators, with four having entered service. In 2007, the TRAI sought to reduce the control of Tata Communications (formerly government-owned VSNL) over international network facilities by requiring the owners of submarine cable landing stations to offer interconnection, co-location, and cable landing services to interested parties on fair and nondiscriminatory terms and conditions. [184] In August 2008, the TRAI authorized ISPs to offer unrestricted IP telephony services. By the end of 2008, approximately 34 ISPs were offering Voice over Internet Protocol (VoIP) services in India. [185]

India has made limited telecommunication service commitments under the GATS. For example, its commitments on market access are recorded as "unbound" for Modes 1, 2, and 4 across more than 10 basic and value-added services. Although India's market access commitments for mode 3 (commercial presence) allow foreign telecommunication operators to enter certain market segments, many such commitments are qualified by licensing and foreign ownership restrictions as well as limitations on the scope of service provision. Similarly, India's national treatment commitments are recorded as unbound for all modes of supply. However, India does include a modified version of the Reference Paper (regulatory principles for telecommunications agreed upon by WTO Members) with its commitments. 186

India's revised offer for the WTO's Doha Round negotiations, submitted in 2005, would substantially liberalize India's bound commitments for telecommunications. India has proposed to remove restrictions on the number of licensed operators, raise foreign equity ceilings, and expand the number of market segments open to foreign telecommunication operators. In addition, India has removed Mode 2 market access and national treatment restrictions for all market segments and added language improving its "Reference Paper" commitments. [187]

With respect to applied measures, foreign investment restrictions for telecommunication services were first relaxed in 2000, when foreign companies were allowed to control a 100 percent equity stake in electronic/voice mail service providers, ISPs without gateway equipment, and dark fiber providers.[188] Starting in 2001, 74 percent foreign ownership was permitted for end-to-end bandwidth services, paging services, and ISPs maintaining gateways.[189] In 2005, the government raised the foreign equity cap from 49 percent to 74 percent for several other services, including fixed-line, mobile, unified access, and DLD/ILD services.[190] In addition to these restrictions, licensing conditions typically require resident Indian citizens to comprise the majority of seats on the Board of Directors.[191]

Competitive Conditions

Fixed-line Services

Historically, the Indian telecommunication services market was served by just two state-owned telecommunication services providers: MTNL, which covered Mumbai and New Delhi, and BSNL, which covered the rest of the country. In addition, India's ILD market was controlled by monopoly provider VSNL (now Tata Communications). Although BSNL and MTNL lost their duopoly in 1997, the main factors facilitating the entrance of new firms in India's fixed-line segment were the liberalization of DLD and ILD markets in 2000 and 2002, respectively; the increase in the foreign equity cap in 2005; and the reduction of licensing fees in 2006.[192]

BSNL remains India's dominant fixed-line operator. Operating in all circles except Mumbai and New Delhi, BSNL had 28 million fixed-line subscribers at the end of 2009, representing approximately 76 percent of the market. Despite such dominance, BSNL has consistently lost market share to rival fixed-line operators over the past few years. Such rivals include MTNL and Bharti Airtel, which controlled 9 and 8 percent of the fixed-line market, respectively, at the end of 2009, as well as Reliance Communications, Tata Telesystems, HFCL Infotel, and Sistema Shyam TeleServices, which each controlled 3 percent or less of the market (table 8).[193]

Table 8. Leading Indian telecommunication service companies

Company	Principal Owners	Services offered
Aircel	Maxis (65%); Apollo Group (35%)	Mobile (5 circles)
Bharat Sanchar Nigam Ltd. (BSNL)	Government (100%)	Fixed-line, mobile (22 circles excluding Mumbai and Delhi), data, Internet
Bharti Airtel	Bharti Telecom Groupa (45%); Pastel Ltdb (16%); Indian Continent Investment Ltdc (6%)	Mobile (22 circles)
HFCL Infotel	Himachal Futuristic Communications Ltd (62%); Birla TMT Holdings (45%); AT Birla Nuvo (36%);	Fixed-line, mobile (1 circle)
Idea Cellular	Hindalco Industries (10%); Grasim Industries (8%)	Mobile (13 circles)
Loop Mobile	BPL Communications (62%); Capital Global (Mauritius) (14%); Gypsy Rover (Mauritius) (17%)	Mobile (Mumbai circle)
Mahanagar Telephone Nigam Ltd. (MTNL)	Government (56%)	Fixed-line, mobile (20 circles), data, Internet, wholesale
Reliance Communications	Anil Dhirubhai Ambani Group (66%)	Fixed-line, mobile (22 circles), Internet
Sistema Shyam TeleServices	Sistema (74%)	Fixed-line, mobile (8 circles)
Spice Communications	Modi Wellvest (51%); Telecom Malaysia (49%)	Mobile (2 circles)
Tata Teleservices	Tata Group (62%); NTT DoCoMo (9%)	Fixed-line, mobile (20 circles), data, Internet, wholesale
Tata Communications (VSNL)	Tata Group (50%); Government (26%)	Fixed-line (International), data, Internet
Vodafone Essar	Vodafone Groupd (52%); Essar Group (33%)	Mobile (22 circles)

Sources: Company Web sites; TeleGeography, India, April 30, 2010; Hot Telecom, Country Profile: India, July 2009.

[a] Bharti Telecom is owned by Bharti Enterprises (63%), Pastel Ltd (33%), and Vodafone (4%).

[b] Pastel Ltd is a wholly-owned subsidiary of Singapore Telecom.

[c] Indian Continent Investment Ltd is a wholly-owned subsidiary of Bharti Enterprises.

[d] Although Vodafone Group (Vodafone) controls approximately 67 percent of Vodafone Essar, and is trying to further increase its stake, it is unable to increase its ownership share in Vodafone Essar because the 33 percent stake held by Essar is structured with 22 percent held offshore, meeting the government of India's 74 percent foreign ownership limitation. The remaining 15 percent of Vodafone Essar is held on behalf of Vodafone by two holding companies affiliated with

Essar, Telecom Investments India Private Ltd. (TIIP) and Omega Telecom Holding Private Ltd. (OTHP). Vodafone Group maintains minority control of TIIP and OTHP, as well as "call options" to acquire 100 percent of shares in the indirect owners of the remainder of the two holding companies. Vodafone also granted "put options" to Essar, exercisable in 2010 and 2011, that allow Essar to sell its entire 33 percent stake to Vodafone for $5 billion.

There were approximately 37 million active fixed telephone lines in India at the end of 2009, resulting in a fixed-line penetration of about 3 percent.[194] During 2009, the total number of fixed lines declined by 2 percent,[195] in line with the average annual decline of 2 percent reported during 2004–08.[196] State-controlled BSNL and MTNL reported net fixed-line losses in 2009, whereas smaller, private sector operators like Bharti Airtel, Reliance Communications, and Tata Teleservices reported net gains.[197] The decline in fixed lines in India is largely explained by the increasing tendency of consumers to substitute mobile telephone service for fixed-line service, a process often referred to as fixed-mobile substitution. In India, fixed-mobile substitution tends to be driven by dissatisfaction with the incumbent fixed-line operators as well as the poor geographic coverage of fixed-line networks. By the end of 2008, fixed line subscribers had fallen to less than 10 percent of India's total telephone subscribers. Although the number of fixed lines is expected to continue to decline, the rate of contraction will likely be mitigated by strong business and corporate demand as well as growing broadband penetration, largely because broadband services are predominantly delivered using fixed-line infrastructure.[198]

Internet Services

Although Internet subscribers in India grew at an annual rate of approximately 24 percent from 2004 through 2008,[199] a subscriber base of 15 million and Internet penetration of approximately 1 percent by the end of 2009 make India one of the world's least-developed Internet markets.[200] In general, the proliferation of Internet services in India is hampered by high levels of poverty, particularly in rural areas, and associated low levels of personal computer ownership.[201] Internet subscriber growth over the past five years has been driven almost entirely by the adoption of residential broadband Internet services, which grew at a CAGR of 153 percent from 135,000 subscribers in 2004 to 5.5 million at the end of 2008.[202] In India, broadband Internet services are predominantly delivered over fixed-line networks (i.e., DSL service), as opposed to delivery via cable television networks. India's Internet services market is in a state of flux, with more than 750 licenses issued over the past few years, while 450 licenses have been revoked. As of December 2008, only about half of India's licensed ISPs had launched Internet services.[203] The top five ISPs in India, measured by market share at the end of 2009, were BSNL (56 percent), MTNL (15 percent), Bharti Airtel (8 percent), Reliance Communications (8 percent), and Hathaway Cable and Datacon (2 percent); all other ISPs each accounted for less than 2 percent of the market.[204]

Mobile Services

India's mobile telephone services market was opened to competition in the early 1990s and has grown rapidly ever since. From 2004 through 2008, for example, mobile subscribers grew at a CAGR of approximately 61 percent.[205] In 2009, the market grew by an additional 51 percent to 525 million subscribers.[206] Such rapid growth, which has made India the world's second-largest mobile services market behind China, can be attributed to falling mobile telephone call prices, the availability of inexpensive handsets, and the expanding reach of mobile networks in rural areas.[207] Despite such rapid growth, however, India's mobile penetration stood at only 45 percent at the end of 2009. Low penetration largely reflects poor mobile network coverage in rural areas, where the majority of India's population lives. In December 2009, mobile penetration in rural areas was approximately 20 percent, compared to 103 percent[208] in urban areas.[209] Such poor coverage has persisted despite the fact that a minimum of three mobile services providers operate in each circle. Mobile operators state that insufficient government financial assistance underlies the poor network coverage in rural areas.[210]

In 2009, the largest mobile provider in India was Bharti Airtel, with a market share of approximately 23 percent, followed by Reliance Communications (18 percent), Vodafone Essar (17 percent), BSNL (12 percent), Idea/Spice Cellular (11 percent), Tata Teleservices (11 percent), and Aircel/Dishnet (6 percent).[211] The DoT's decision to issue UAS licenses provided a major boost to competition in India's mobile market, as Reliance Communications and Tata Teleservices, among others, began to rapidly expand network coverage and compete for new subscribers.[212] By mid-2010, the entry of so many new firms into India's mobile services market had sparked a debilitating price war, with per-minute tariffs falling to less than one

U.S. cent per minute. Although falling per-minute prices have been welcomed by consumers, the decline in industry revenue has had a catastrophic effect on India's telecommunication service operators. As of March 2010, for example, large operators in India had experienced a fall in average monthly revenue per user of 38 percent. Fierce competition also led UK-based Vodafone to write down the value of its investment in Vodafone Essar by $3.3 billion, or more than 25 percent. Indeed, competition in India's mobile market is such that some of the smaller operators may not survive.[213]

Under such conditions, many experts believe that industry consolidation is necessary to reduce the number of competing firms, but existing rules effectively prevent such consolidation.[214] In particular, telecom operators are not allowed to buy out a rival operating in the same circle, as rules restrict operators to one license per circle. In addition, telecom operators are not allowed to own more than 10 percent of another operator or sell a majority stake in a telecommunication services company within the first three years of obtaining a license.[215] In response to concerns that the Indian mobile sector is overcrowded, the TRAI has recommended to the government that mergers and acquisitions be allowed, provided that at least six companies will be operating in each circle following any deal and that the merged entity will not control more than 30 percent of the total user base in each circle.[216] Relatively recent regulatory actions promise to further intensify price-based competition in India's mobile services market. For example, following the DoT's 2007 decision to license all interested companies, several existing mobile operators—Tata Teleservices, Reliance, Vodafone Essar, and Aircel, among others— were approved to expand, in some cases significantly, the number of circles in which they operate. Following the receipt of licenses, several new firms have launched commercial services, including Loop Telecom, Etisalat DB, and Unitech Wireless.

Additionally, in March 2009, the DoT agreed to authorize the provision of mobile services by mobile virtual network operators (MVNOs),[217] a move that is expected to attract additional new entrant companies. The government's decision to implement mobile number portability in 2010 also promises to increase competition as mobile operators attempt to retain existing customers while simultaneously luring new customers away from rival firms.[218] Other factors that may sharpen price competition in India's mobile market include price sensitivity among low-income and rural consumers, market segments that are increasingly targeted by mobile operators, and the lack of differentiation in network quality and customer service.[219]

As competition and government-imposed termination rate cuts continue to erode profit margins, many mobile operators are developing value-added services (VAS) as a way to differentiate service offerings and drive future revenue growth. Currently, the most popular VAS products revolve around India's prominent film industry. Catering mainly to the youth market, such products include ringtones of popular Bollywood songs, wallpapers featuring leading actors, and games with movie themes.[220]

In April 2010, following more than two years of delays, the DoT launched an auction to allocate electromagnetic spectrum, on a circle-by-circle basis, among nine pre-approved telecommunication service operators.[221] Such spectrum is intended to support the rollout of third generation (3G) services (high-speed Internet and other data services delivered via mobile telephone handsets). After more than 34 days of bidding, seven operators obtained licenses, although no single operator was able to obtain licenses in all 22 circles. Three companies—Bharti Airtel, Reliance Communications, and Aircel—managed to acquire 2 x 5 MHz paired spectrum in 13 circles for $2.7 billion, $1.8 billion, and $1.4 billion, respectively. Idea Cellular obtained licenses in 11 circles, while Tata Teleservices and Vodafone Essar each obtained licenses in 9 circles; S Tel, in 2 circles.[222] State-controlled operators BSNL and MTNL were each allocated 3G spectrum in 2009, on the condition that each company would pay the winning bid price for each circle.[223] It is estimated that the government of India will receive nearly $14.5 billion from the auction.[224]

Many analysts, observers, and industry participants believe that auction design and high levels of competition resulted in very high prices for 3G licenses relative to India's level of economic development.[225] Although access to such spectrum is necessary for the development of 3G services, many observers believe that the expense of such services places them beyond the means of most of the Indian population. As a result, winning operators will likely use much of their spectrum allocation, at least initially, to relieve existing network capacity constraints, supporting further growth in basic voice service subscribers.[226]

Foreign Investment and International Trade

India's telecommunication services industry has attracted significant foreign investment over the past several years, with foreign investors entering the market through both strategic acquisitions and joint venture arrangements.

Attracted by the prospect of high subscriber and revenue growth rates, India's mobile market has been particularly popular with foreign investors, mainly foreign telecommunication companies. In 2005, for example, Malaysia-based Maxis Communications purchased 65 percent of Aircel for $1.1 billion. In 2007, the United Kingdom's Vodafone paid $11 billion for 65 percent of Hutchison Essar, renaming it Vodafone Essar. In 2008, Russian telecommunications giant Sistema purchased 74 percent of Shyam Telelink, while UAE-based Etisalat purchased a 45-percent stake in Swan Telecom for $900 million. In 2009, Bahrain Telecommunications Company (Batelco) acquired a 49-percent stake in S Tel, Singapore Telecommunications announced plans to increase its indirect stake in Bharti Airtel to 32 percent, and the government of India authorized Telenor (Norway) to increase its stake in Unitech Wireless from 49 percent to 67 percent.[227]

The DLD and ILD markets are also popular with foreign telecommunication companies. In April 2007, for example, U.S.-based AT&T, in partnership with domestic automobile manufacturer Mahindra & Mahindra, became the first foreign telecommunications company to offer domestic and international long distance services in India.[228] Similarly, the United Kingdom's BT was awarded DLD and ILD licenses in 2007. Aiming to serve international corporations in India, BT signed an agreement with BSNL that will allow it to offer managed services, including basic telecommunication services as well as leased-line, Internet, mobile, and broadband services. In 2008, Verizon (United States) and Cable & Wireless (United Kingdom) also received DLD/ILD licenses from the DoT. Verizon, which also holds an ISP license, plans to offer DLD/ILD services through a joint venture with Mumbai-based Videocon Group, whereas Cable & Wireless plans to offer services to corporate clients through a joint venture with TTK Group.[229] In November 2009, Australia's Telstra applied to India's Foreign Investment Promotion Board for permission to increase its stake in Indian operator Telstra Communications from 49 percent to 74 percent. Subject to approval, Telstra plans to acquire DLD/ILD licenses as well as an ISP concession from the DoT.[230]

Indian telecommunication service providers are also beginning to invest in the telecommunication markets of other countries. In March 2010, for example, Bharti Airtel purchased the mobile service operations of Zain Group (Kuwait) in 15 African countries for $10.7 billion. Similarly, in January 2010, Bharti Airtel agreed to pay $1.0 billion for a 70 percent stake in Bangladeshi services provider Warid Telecom. [231] BSNL and MTNL have also indicated an interest in acquiring telecommunication companies outside of India, particularly in Africa.[232] Efforts on the part of Indian operators to expand abroad will likely continue, driven by factors including strong balance sheet positions, the existence of growth opportunities in many emerging markets, and an expected decline in Indian growth rates starting in 2012 or 2013. Expansion efforts will likely continue to focus on Africa and the Middle East as Indian operators attempt to transplant business models that were successful in India to countries with similar regulatory and demographic characteristics.[233]

In India, as in most countries, the primary form of cross-border trade in telecommunication services is a standard international telephone call that originates in India and terminates in a foreign country, and vice versa. In 2008, India's outgoing telephone traffic totaled approximately 5.2 billion minutes, an increase of roughly 24 percent over the previous year. The largest share of India's outgoing telephone traffic terminated in the United States (31 percent), followed by Saudi Arabia (13 percent), the United Arab Emirates (10 percent), the United Kingdom (7 percent), and Qatar (5 percent). While the increase in outgoing traffic was impressive, the increase in incoming traffic was even more so—it jumped 30 percent over the previous year to 15.2 billion minutes.[234] In 2008, U.S. exports of telecommunication services to India totaled approximately $139 million, while imports totaled $331 million, yielding a U.S. trade deficit of $192 million.[235]

In addition to the foreign equity restrictions already discussed, U.S. companies have noted several other nontariff barriers in India's telecommunication services market. In the DLD/ILD market, for example, U.S. companies have cited licensing fees of approximately $500,000 per service as a barrier to market entry for small telecommunication service companies. U.S. firms have also noted that the Indian government's ownership positions in BSNL and MTNL may be affecting the fairness of telecommunication services policies. In particular, U.S. firms are concerned about the government's policy of setting aside wireless frequency spectrum for BSNL and MTNL in connection with India's electromagnetic spectrum auction. The U.S. telecommunications industry also objects to India's licensing requirement for companies offering VoIP services that terminate on public switched networks, stating that such requirements are overly burdensome for small companies that specialize in VoIP services.[236] Lastly, in August 2009, the *Financial Times* reported that the DoT was considering, at the request of state security agencies, a requirement that senior management positions in telecommunication services companies be filled with Indian nationals, largely over concerns that non-Indian senior managers would have the ability to authorize the monitoring and interception of telephone calls.[237]

ENERGY SERVICES

Overview

In 2007, India was the fifth largest electricity producer in the world, behind the United States, China, Japan, and Russia (table 9). Between 2006 and 2007, India increased the quantity of electricity it produced by more than any other country in the world, aside from China.238 Demand, however, has increased at an even faster rate, resulting in a shortage of electricity and frequent power outages during peak hours.239 In addition to a shortage of generation capacity, India faces significant challenges in electricity transmission and distribution. Due to the lack of an integrated national transmission system, India sometimes experiences simultaneous electricity surpluses in some areas and deficits in others. In 2007, India lost 198 billion kilowatt-hours due to distribution losses, which was more than double the total electricity production of neighboring Pakistan. These losses accounted for 26 percent of total electricity output, which is nearly three times the global average for distribution losses.240 Additionally, in 2007, India's per capita consumption of electricity was lower than the average for every region in the world except South Asia.

Table 9. Largest electricity producing countries, 2007

Country	Net generation (million kilowatt-hours)	Net generation CAGR, 03–07 (%)	Imports (% of total consumption)	Exports (% of total generation)	Losses (% of total output)
United States	4,157	2	1.31	0.49	6
China	3,041	14	0.17	0.46	6
Japan	1,058	2	0.00	0.00	5
Russia	958	3	0.67	1.93	10
India	762	6	0.87	0.03	25
World	18,779	4	3.64	3.33	8

Sources: USDOE, EIA, International Energy Statistics database; World Bank, WDI Online database (both accessed May 17, 2010).

This likely reflects India's relatively low level of urbanization compared to other lower-middle-income countries, among other factors.241 The consequences of these inadequacies for industries and individuals are severe. Electrical equipment is damaged and burns out more quickly as a result of outages and fluctuating voltage, workers are idled during blackouts, and businesses need to invest in costly diesel generators.[242]

The Indian government, recognizing that the lack of sufficient electricity supplies has acted as a constraint on economic growth, has implemented a number of reforms in recent years in an attempt to increase the efficiency and capacity of the country's electricity industry. These initiatives, however, have met with mixed success due to India's complex political and regulatory structure.[243]

The Indian electricity industry is dominated by public sector entities. The federal government controls about 32 percent of generation capacity in India, and state electricity boards (SEBs) control an additional 55 percent, leaving only about 13 percent of generation in private hands.[244] Additionally, the transmission and distribution subsectors are entirely state-owned in all but a few states.[245]

Although imports of certain fuel sources (box 2), such as natural gas, are important to the Indian electricity market, trade in electricity, either through cross-border trade or affiliate transactions, accounts for only a small fraction of the electricity consumed in India. Since cross-border electricity trade requires physical transmission lines, countries' ability to trade electricity with adjacent countries depends heavily on geography and political cooperation. While India's power grid is interconnected with those of neighboring Nepal and Bhutan, India's imports totaled less than 1 percent of total consumption in 2007.[246] The country's cross-border exports of electricity were even smaller, accounting for only 0.03 percent of total generation.[247]

**Box 2. Fuel sources, generation technologies,
and the Indian electricity market**

India's ability to significantly expand its electricity generation capacity hinges on securing sufficient quantities of affordably priced fuel and generation technologies. However, each major fuel source and generation technology at India's disposal is associated with unique policy and/or technical challenges.

Coal is India's most important fuel source for electricity generation, accounting for approximately 70 percent of total electric production. India is the world's third-largest coal producer and has an abundant supply of domestic coal, but also imports significant quantities from Indonesia, Australia, and South Africa.[a] Domestic coal production is controlled by a state-owned monopoly which historically has not invested heavily in production.[b] There are concerns inside and outside the country about the environmental implications of increasing the use of coal, given that Indian coal has a high ash content and is therefore less efficient and more polluting than other types of coal.[c]

Natural gas was the fastest growing fuel source for electric production in India in the early 2000s due to the relatively low capital costs of building natural gas-fired generation facilities, among other factors. Domestically produced natural gas accounts for the majority of consumption in the country, although imports have grown at a significantly faster rate than domestic production since 2004.[d] In recent years, however, India has faced severe shortages of natural gas, which has caused the share of power generated from natural gas to decline and has lead to the scaling back of plans to add a significant amount of natural gas-fired generation capacity.[e]

Nuclear power currently plays a minor role in Indian electricity production, accounting for just 3 percent of total generation capacity. While the Indian government has placed a high priority on expanding its nuclear power capacity, India has relatively small domestic reserves of low-grade uranium, making nuclear power sourced from indigenous uranium more expensive and less efficient than in other countries.[f] India's ability to import uranium and nuclear technology was severely limited before 2008 because of restrictions placed on India by foreign suppliers due to its refusal to sign the Nuclear Non-Proliferation Treaty.

However, in October 2008, the U.S. Congress approved an agreement which paved the way for greater Indian access to international supplies of nuclear fuels and technologies.[g]

Renewable sources represent a small but growing share of India's power generation portfolio. Hydropower is the largest renewable source by far. The Indian government estimates that the country has significant unused hydroelectric potential and has consequently announced plans to dramatically increase hydroelectric capacity.[h] However, opposition to certain large hydroelectric projects due to perceived negative environmental and social impacts may hinder these initiatives.[i] India is currently the world's fifth-largest wind energy producer, with over 10,000 MW of installed capacity as of July 2009 and estimates of potential capacity as high as 65,000 MW. However, wind's intermittent nature limits its contribution to the country's overall power generation.[j] Additionally, both the national and state governments are supporting the growth of solar power with a variety of subsidies and incentive programs.[k]

[a] USDOE, EIA, "India: Electricity," March 2009; EIU, "India Coal," June 12, 2009.
[b] EIU, "India Coal," June 12, 2009.
[c] EIU, "India: Energy Report," May 26, 2009.
[d] USDOE, EIA, "India: Natural Gas," March 2009.
[e] World Bank, WDI Online database (accessed September 8, 2009); Scully, Global Industry Surveys, April 2007, 3.
[f] Government of India, Planning Commission, Integrated Energy Policy, August 2006, 35; Mukherjee and Goswami, "Trade in Energy Services," January 2009, 26.
[g] Pan and Bajoria, "The U.S.-India Nuclear Deal," October 2, 2008.
[h] Government of India, Planning Commission, Integrated Energy Policy, August 2006, 37–38.
[i] USDOE, EIA, "India: Electricity," March 2009.
[j] Indian Wind Energy Association Web site, http://www.inwea.org (accessed September 10, 2009); EIU, "India Alternatives," May 5, 2009.
[k] EIU, "India Alternatives," May 5, 2009.

As of 2007, only two multinational electric power utilities operated in the Indian power market: AES (United States), which owns a minority share in one 420 megawatt (MW) coal plant, and China Light and Power Holdings Ltd. (Hong Kong), which owns and operates a 655 MW gas-fired combined cycle power station.[248] Combined, these two operations accounted for less than 1 percent of total Indian generation capacity in 2007.[249] There is, however, U.S. and other foreign portfolio investment in a number of Indian electricity firms, including NTPC, the largest public sector power generation company, and Tata Power, the largest private one.[250]

Factors Affecting Supply and Demand

India's power shortages are largely a function of its policy environment. Although the national government plays a major role in setting the country's energy policy and in direct provision of electricity, the states set many of the most important policies affecting the sector, including the establishment of electricity prices. Most states have enacted rate schemes that provide electricity below cost to a number of important constituencies, including households and farmers. Several states provide electricity to farmers free of charge.[251] Lower rates for certain categories of electricity consumers come at the expense of other classes of consumers and state budgets. The rates that Indian households pay for electricity are significantly lower than the OECD average, while the rates that Indian industry pays are significantly higher than the OECD average.[252] Nearly all of the state electricity boards are technically bankrupt and, in many states, electricity subsidies are the largest single drain on state revenues.[253] The bankrupt SEBs lack the funds needed to invest in additional generation capacity and to maintain and expand their transmission and distribution infrastructure. This poor infrastructure deters private investment in generation, because private generators must rely on SEB-owned grids to purchase and distribute the electricity they generate.[254]

The Indian government has undertaken a number of reforms in recent years in order to address some of the critical shortcomings in the electricity sector. The 2003 Electricity Act sought to increase private investment in the electricity sector, reduce the influence of state governments over regulators, increase competition in the marketplace, and gradually reduce the rate subsidies for some electricity consumers. The Act also required the SEBs to create separate legal entities for generation, transmission, and distribution, and to allow private participation in each of these segments.[255] However, implementation of these reforms has progressed fairly slowly and unevenly, as some states have been much more aggressive in reforming their electricity markets than others. For instance, most states have established independent electricity regulators, but relatively few have privatized significant portions of their electricity industries.[256] Additionally, few states have made significant progress in reducing cross-subsidization of electricity tariffs, although the national government has stipulated that by 2011, states will have to significantly reduce the degree to which different groups of consumers pay vastly different rates.[257]

AIR TRANSPORT SERVICES

Overview

India's air passenger transport market is relatively small, accounting for only 2 percent of airline traffic worldwide.[258] In 2007, Indian airlines transported approximately 53 million passengers, more than 80 percent of whom were domestic travelers.[259] During the same year, operating revenue for India's air transport industry was roughly $7.2 billion, and the number of workers employed in the sector reached nearly 60,000.[260] Although India's air transport industry experienced substantial growth over the past five years, such growth has been slowed by the recent financial crisis. During the period 2002–06, the number of passengers transported on Indian airlines increased at an average annual rate of 15 percent. Passenger growth accelerated to more than 20 percent during 2007–08.[261] However, in the first half of 2009, passenger traffic in India reportedly decreased by 8 percent.[262] Similarly, operating revenues for India's air transport sector declined by an estimated $2 billion in 2008, after increasing by a total of $3.7 billion between 2002 and 2007.[263] Despite the current downturn, growth potential remains as the young and increasingly affluent Indian population selects air transport over other modes of domestic travel.[264]

Box 3. Air freight services in India experience growth

India's air freight market is growing rapidly, driven principally by increasing merchandise trade between India and foreign countries. In 2008, India's share of the global air freight market was less than 1 percent by volume, but grew by 15 percent over the previous year.[a] Overall, India's air freight market is forecast to expand by an average of more than 8 percent per year through 2011, making it the second largest market, after China, in terms of annual growth.[b] At present, the majority of air cargo in India is transported by passenger airlines.

In 2007, the total revenues earned by Indian passenger airlines for the transport of freight were $170 million.[c] During the same year, Jet Airways accounted for the largest share of India's air freight market by volume at 31 percent, followed by Indian Airlines, 23 percent, and Blue Dart Express, an all-cargo carrier, 18 percent.[d] Air cargo carriers serve an increasingly important role in India's freight transport market, particularly for time-sensitive shipments that are moved less efficiently by road and rail. In addition to Blue Dart Express, several new cargo airlines have emerged within India to meet increasing demand for air freight services, including Deccan Express Limited, Flyington Freighters, and QuickJet.[e]

The government has liberalized foreign investment in domestic air freight services, permitting foreign airlines to own up to a 74 percent equity stake in Indian cargo airlines. India maintains an "open skies" policy on air freight transport, enabling foreign airlines to serve India's growing international air cargo market.[f] Nonetheless, air cargo carriers operating in India face infrastructure constraints, including lack of adequate storage and warehousing facilities at airports. To aid the growth of India's air freight services sector, the government has constructed the country's first cargo and logistics hub in the centrally-located city of Nagpur and plans to build additional air cargo terminals throughout India.

[a] Directorate General of Civil Aviation, Statistical Division, India Air Transport Statistics, 2007–08, April 2009, 27.
[b] IATA, "Passenger and Freight Forecasts 2007 to 2011," October 2007, 4.
[c] Directorate General of Civil Aviation, "Financial Results of Scheduled Domestic Private Airlines of India," n.d. Data on freight revenues is reported for the period ending March 31, 2008, and does not include freight revenues earned by India's national airlines.
[d] Directorate General of Civil Aviation, Statistical Division, India Air Transport Statistics, 2007–08, April 2009, 27.
[e] Narayanan, "India Poised for Air Cargo Revolution," September 2009.
[f] Narayanan, "India Poised for Air Cargo Revolution," September 2009. Open skies agreements remove restrictions on the routes that airlines from signatory countries can fly and the frequency of their service. However, open skies agreements do not permit signatories' airlines to provide cabotage, or domestic point-to-point transport service, within each other's countries.
[g] ArabianBusiness.com, "India Ministry Plans Cargo Airports," April 1, 2007.

India's air passenger transport market primarily comprises three government-owned and six privately owned airlines (table 10). The largest of these, in terms of operating revenue, is the national carrier, Air India, which in August 2007 merged with another government-owned carrier, Indian Air, to form the National Aviation Company of India.[265] In 2008, Air India had a 16 percent share of the country's domestic air passenger transport market.[266] Among India's largest privately owned airlines, Jet Airways and Kingfisher operate the most extensive air transport networks and compete directly with Air India. [267] The remaining four private carriers are considered "low-cost" airlines and operate domestic routes only.[268] In 2008, Jet Airways had the highest share of India's domestic air passenger market at 22 percent.[269] Indian airlines do not compete with foreign carriers on the country's domestic routes, as the latter are not permitted to operate within India's domestic air transport market.[270] However, Air India, Jet Airways, and Kingfisher face strong competition from non-Indian airlines for service between India and foreign countries.

Table 10. Major airlines in India, 2008[a]

Airline	Ownership	Routes	Operating revenues ($ million)	Profit (Loss) ($ million)
Air India	Public	Domestic and international	1,700[b]	(255)[b]
Air India Express	Public	Domestic and international	162b	3[b]
Indian Airlines	Public	Domestic	1,200[b]	(289)[b]
Alliance Air	Public	Domestic	79[b]	(18)[b]
Go Airways	Private	Domestic	106	(36)
Indigo Airlines	Private	Domestic	236	(49)
Jet Airways	Private	Domestic and international	1,800	(53)
Kingfisher Airlines	Private	Domestic and international	560	(85)
Paramount Airways	Private	Domestic	53[b]	5[b]
SpiceJet Airlines	Private	Domestic	270	(28)

Source: Directorate General of Civil Aviation, "Airline-wise Financial Status of All Scheduled Indian Carriers (2001– 2002 to 2003–2004 to 2006–2007)"; Directorate General of Civil Aviation, "Financial Results of Scheduled Domestic Private Airlines of India (2007–2008)"; IndiaStat, "Profit and Loss of Selected Airlines of India (2005–2006 to 2007– 2008)."
[a]Data from the year ending March 31, 2008, unless otherwise specified.
[b]Data from the year ending March 31, 2007.

For instance, in 2005, more than half of air passengers traveling between India and the United Kingdom were transported on airlines based in the Middle East, such as Emirates and Gulf Air.[271]

In the past two years, India's airline industry has consolidated in order to reduce excess capacity and streamline costs. For example, prior to the merger of Air India and Indian Air, Jet Airways purchased Air Sahara in April 2007, and Kingfisher Airlines acquired a 46 percent stake in low-cost carrier Air Deccan in June 2007.[272] Jet Airways' purchase of Air Sahara enabled the former to expand its international routes and created the largest privately operated airline in India.[273] By contrast, Kingfisher's acquisition of Air Deccan allowed Kingfisher to compete in India's domestic, low-fare passenger market.[274] Despite these mergers, Indian airlines still face lower labor productivity and higher costs than non-Indian airlines. In 2008, the average number of employees per aircraft on Indian domestic carriers was 169, compared to 125 employees on U.S. and European airlines.[275] In addition, the Indian government reportedly places relatively high taxes on jet fuel and imposes high airport usage fees on air carriers, both of which make the operation of Indian airlines less cost-effective than that of foreign airlines.[276]

India's Participation in Global Trade

India's share of global trade in air passenger transport services is small. In 2006, India's global exports of air passenger transport services totaled $280 million, compared to $2.8 billion for China and $22 billion for the United States. Similarly, India's global imports of air passenger transport services in 2006 were $1.9 billion, significantly less than the $3.9 billion recorded for China, and far below the $27 billion registered for the United States.[277]

In 2008, U.S. exports of air passenger transport services to India reached nearly $1.3 billion, making India the second-largest market for U.S. exports in this industry in the Asia-Pacific region and the seventh-largest market worldwide. By contrast, U.S. imports of air passenger transport services from India registered only $323 million.[278] The high volume of U.S. exports of air passenger transport services to India reflects the number of Indian business travelers, students, and tourists traveling to the United States from India on U.S. airlines. Although U.S. imports of air passenger transport services from India in 2008 were low, U.S. tourism expenditures in India were relatively high, suggesting that the majority of U.S. residents that traveled to India did so on non-Indian airlines.[279]

India has made no commitments for air transport services under the GATS. Presently, foreign equity participation of up to 49 percent is permitted in India's domestic air transport industry by non-airline entities,[280] but foreign airlines have been prohibited from purchasing shares in India's passenger airlines since the late 1990s. For instance, in 1993, India's largest privately owned carrier, Jet Airways, was established with a combined 40 percent equity share from Bahrain-based Gulf Air and Kuwait Airways, but the two airlines were directed by the Indian Government to divest their shares in 1997.[281]

India's latest offer for the Doha Round of global trade negotiations would not commit India to significant liberalization of the industry, as its section on air transport addresses only aircraft maintenance and repair.[282] However, in light of the recent poor financial performance of the industry, the government is reportedly considering permitting foreign carriers to own up to a 25 percent stake in Indian passenger airlines.[283]

Factors Affecting Supply and Demand

The supply of air transport services in India has been primarily influenced by government privatization and liberalization of the sector and new investment in air transport infrastructure. Privatization of India's air transport sector, through which the government ended its monopoly on domestic air service by permitting the entry of Indian-owned private-sector carriers, was formalized in 1994.[284] Prior to 1994, however, the government began granting a select number of licenses to private carriers operating in the Indian market, including Jet Airways and its current subsidiary, Air Sahara.[285] By 1996, Indian-owned private airlines reportedly accounted for a 43 percent share of India's domestic air passenger market.[286] Since then, and particularly in the past five years, growth in the demand for domestic air travel has led to the entry of additional carriers and a significant increase in airline capacity. Between 2003 and 2006, 13 new private airlines entered India's aviation market, including Go Air, Indigo, Kingfisher, Paramount Airways, and SpiceJet. During this period, the number of passengers transported by private airlines in India more than doubled, while growth in the passenger volume of India's national airlines remained relatively flat.[287] By late 2005, private airlines accounted for a 68 percent share of India's domestic air passenger market.[288]

The addition of new airline capacity in India has also stimulated public investment in airport infrastructure. The Indian government is currently upgrading four of India's largest airports—Chennai, Delhi, Kolkata, and Mumbai—and has constructed two new airports—Bangalore and Hyderabad[289]— with the aid of private sector investment.[290] Such investments are viewed as necessary to support the growth of India's air transport industry and facilitate the country's increasing participation in international trade and tourism. For example, in terms of passenger traffic, Delhi's airport is currently operating at twice the capacity for which it was designed. The government plans to expand the airport's capacity to handle 40 million passengers per year by 2010 and 100 million passengers per year by 2026.[291]

Demand for air transport services in India has been greatly affected by the expansion of the country's middle class, as well as growth in India's tourism market. The middle class, which is relatively young and well-educated, has contributed to increased domestic demand for both business and leisure travel.[292] Although rail transport has traditionally served as the primary mode of travel within India, air transport has grown in popularity, in large part due to the entry of low-cost airlines into India's aviation market.[293] Still, more than 95 percent of India's population has never traveled by air.[294] Based on estimates of the potential demand for air transport among the country's more than one billion residents, some predict that India will become one of the world's fastest growing markets for air transport.[295]

India is also experiencing strong growth in international air travel. During the period 2003–07, the number of foreign tourists traveling in India increased at an average annual rate of approximately 16 percent, as did the number Indian tourists traveling abroad. This was significantly higher than the rate of growth in Indian inbound and outbound tourism during the previous five-year period.[296] Bilateral air services agreements between India and foreign countries have helped facilitate international tourism to India, as well as Indian travel abroad. India has concluded 103 bilateral air services agreements to date, greatly expanding the number of countries to which Indian airlines may fly. Most recently, in September 2008, India signed new bilateral air services agreements with Mexico and Chile, and concluded a horizontal air services agreement with the European Communities.[297]

EDUCATION SERVICES

Overview

India's higher education system has the world's largest number of institutions (approximately 21,500 in 2008, up from 11,400 in 2000) and its third-largest number of students (about 15 million in 2008, up from 9 million in 2000).[298] Nevertheless, both the quantity and quality of services supplied by India's higher education system are insufficient to meet demand from eligible students and their prospective employers. A small portion of India's higher education institutions is renowned for producing graduates who are adequately prepared for advanced degree programs, research, or employment in scientific, technological, or commercial fields in India and abroad. However, most of India's universities and colleges lack the financial resources, authority, and flexibility to equip graduates with the skills demanded by India's expanding business and technology sectors. Many students from India, therefore, pursue higher education opportunities abroad.

With about two-thirds of the population of India under age 25, national and state government funding priorities for education for the 20-year period through 2005 centered on increasing participation in elementary education (grades 1 through 5), especially among the population segments with relatively low levels of participation in education. Despite India's progress in recent years in making elementary education more available—especially to historically underrepresented segments such as girls, children in eastern India, and culturally disadvantaged groups—substantial numbers of students continue to exit the education system at every level.[299] As a result, only about 12 percent of 18- to 24-year-olds in India had enough prior education to advance to higher education in 2005.

The central government's 11th five-year plan (2007–12) elevated the policy and fiscal priorities of higher education relative to other levels of education. Programs to be implemented under the current plan include doubling the number of India's elite higher education institutions and creating new central government-funded universities in Indian states currently lacking such institutions. In 2009, the central government announced that expenditures on higher education would increase by 55 percent over the previous fiscal year.[300]

India's approximately 500 universities vary in origin and character, yet they share the nearly exclusive legal authority to grant degrees recognized throughout India.[301] They can be divided into three primary categories: (1) those formed as the result of acts of the Indian Parliament (approximately 24 central universities) or state legislatures (about 251 state universities); (2) those that have received the central government's authorization to award degrees by achieving the status of "deemed-to-be universities"[302] (at least 104 institutions); and (3) those that have been designated by Parliament as "institutions of national importance." The Indian Institutes of Technology (IITs) head the third category as the country's most prestigious higher education institutions. Open universities are another type of Indian university, providing degrees and programs mostly through online instruction. The most important is Indira Gandhi National Open University (IGNOU), with over 2 million students (about 15 percent of all students in higher education in India) enrolled in January 2009.[303] IGNOU provides education services[304] through a network of regional centers throughout the country, while all other open universities in India supply education services to students only within single states.

The vast majority of the estimated 21,000 colleges in India are affiliates of Indian universities. Universities grant affiliation status to colleges in consultation with state governments, determine courses of study and instructional norms and procedures at the colleges, and award degrees.[305]

Technical education at numerous types of post-secondary institutions is of particular importance in producing skilled labor and enhancing industrial production in India. Principal funding for these institutions comes from the central or state governments or through self-financing. Central government funds support more than 50 technical institutions, including IITs, Indian Institutes of Management (IIMs), and others, which provide postgraduate research programs, degree programs, and nondegree courses and programs in engineering technology, management, architecture, town planning, pharmacology, hotel management, and other fields.[306]

About 31 percent of enrollment in Indian higher education is in private institutions.[307] In recent years, new private colleges and a small number of private universities (unaided by government funding) accounted for most of the increase in higher education institutions in India. For example, from FY 2000– 2001 through FY 2005–06, private, unaided institutions more than doubled in number and also increased as a share of all colleges and universities in India, from 25 percent to 43 percent during the period.[308] Constraints on central and state government funding of higher education, evidenced by annual decreases in real public expenditures per student from 2000 through 2006, led many Indian state governments to recognize new private institutions,[309] especially those that provide engineering, medical, and management degrees or that prepare students for employment in information technology.[310]

Participation in Global Trade

In every year from 2002 through 2008, India ranked as the leading market for U.S. exports of education services. In 2008, U.S. education services exports to India reached $2.7 billion, vastly surpassing the United States' $46 million in imports of education services from India. Education services exports to India accounted for 15 percent of total U.S. exports of education services in 2008, up from 10 percent in 2002, after more than doubling from 2002 through

2008 and increasing at an average annual rate of 14 percent. Such exports accounted for 25 percent of total U.S. exports of services to India in 2008, lower than the 38 percent share that education services contributed to total U.S. services exports to India in 2002.[311]

Indian trade in education services continues to expand. From 2002 through 2007, the number of Indian students enrolled in universities abroad grew to about 153,300, up 24 percent from the start of the period. India accounted for the second-largest number of students enrolled at foreign universities, following China, in 2002 through 2007. The United States is the leading destination for Indians studying abroad. In 2007, 56 percent of Indian students who enrolled in universities outside of India did so at U.S. institutions (about 86,000 students), while universities in Australia and the United Kingdom each accounted for about 16 percent of Indian students enrolled abroad. However, in recent years, Australian and British universities have enrolled students from India at a much faster rate than have U.S. universities,[312] in part because of the expanded availability and marketing of scholarships to Indian students engaged in graduate-level research programs at these countries' universities. In contrast, the reduced availability of financial aid from U.S. universities to Indian students has contributed to decreases in the enrollment of graduate students from India.[313]

Few Indian universities engage in marketing activities to attract foreign students and the government of India has provided limited support for this purpose.[314] In 2008, approximately 21,200 foreign students enrolled in universities in India, up from about 13,300 in 2005. Less than 400 students from the United States (2 percent of all students from abroad) enrolled in Indian universities in 2008, 36 percent fewer than the number of U.S. students enrolled in 2007.[315]

Foreign universities and colleges are not permitted to establish branch campuses as universities in India or to confer degrees recognized officially in India.[316] Instead, foreign universities chiefly offer vocational or technical programs, or collaborate with Indian institutions in various degree and nondegree programs, research endeavors, or course delivery arrangements[317] under which the Indian partner awards degrees recognized in India. The most common type of collaborative arrangement is "twinning," whereby Indian students attend portions of their studies at institutions in India as well as abroad and earn degrees recognized in both countries. The foreign university establishes the curriculum and determines the instructional materials, lecture content, and examinations for each course in the degree program, whether taught at the Indian or foreign institution.

In recent years, a limited number of higher education institutions and education firms from India have established branch campuses or other instructional facilities abroad. Since 2000, several India-based institutions have established degree programs in Dubai, United Arab Emirates (UAE): Birla Institute of Technology and Science (BITS-Pilani) and Manipal Education offer bachelor's and master's degrees in science and engineering fields, while S.P. Jain Center of Management and the Institute of Management and Technology established management programs. S.P. Jain also operates a campus in Singapore, as does the Indian Institute of Management Bangalore. In addition, Manipal Education has acquired medical colleges in Malaysia, Nepal, and Antigua.[318]

Although India has made no binding commitments for education services under the GATS, the country submitted a conditional offer of commitments for higher education services in the Doha Round negotiations in 2005. The offer would place no limitations on market access for higher education services trade when supplied in its most prevalent form (mode 2, consumption abroad), which applies when persons reside abroad temporarily for the purpose of formal study at a foreign educational institution. India's offer also would not limit access by foreign entities seeking to deliver such services in India under mode 1 (cross-border supply), as long as such entities are subject to regulations as may apply in the country of origin of such services. Moreover, India's offer would not limit access under mode 3 (commercial presence), except under conditions related to the establishment of fees and investment approval requirements of the Foreign Investment Promotion Board. India offered full national treatment commitments (without limitations) under modes 1, 2, and 3. The market access and national treatment limitations pertaining to mode 4 (presence of natural persons) would parallel those applicable to all services included in India's conditional offer.[319]

Developments in Regulation and Quality

India's central government has ultimate authority on policy issues and regulation of higher education and exercises this authority through several regulatory agencies with overlapping jurisdictions. Although the Ministry of Human Resource Development has primary responsibility for the sector, at least 15 other central government ministries or departments are involved in the oversight or financing of higher education.[320] The University Grants Commission (UGC), a statutory body of the Ministry of Human Resource

Development, has broad authority over universities and colleges in India. Its principal functions include determining and coordinating standards of instruction, examination, and research; evaluating institutions' suitability for recognition; allocating and disbursing grants; and advising central and state governments on measures necessary to further develop higher education.[321] The All India Council for Technical Education (AICTE), another major statutory body in the Ministry of Human Resource Development, oversees planning and development of diverse institutions that provide technical education in India.[322] Further, regulatory councils established under various statutes aim to ensure the quality of education in various professions in India by setting minimum standards for an institution's recognition and by requiring council pre-approval to establish a new institution to teach professionals.

The Indian regulatory system for higher education has long been the subject of comprehensive study and recommendations for change. Education experts have raised concerns about overlapping functions among the central and state government regulatory authorities, as well as governmental control over tuition and fees, curriculum approvals, student admissions policies, faculty and staff salaries, and administrator appointments, all of which compromise the autonomy and minimize the authority of higher education institutions. In recent years, the Indian government has examined recommendations by commissions of experts concerning the replacement of the current, fragmented regulatory system with a single, central government regulatory agency.[323] Recent regulatory changes aim to provide increased coordination and more precise delineation of responsibilities among several regulatory bodies concerning distance (online) education in India.[324]

The quality of India's higher education institutions varies considerably. Government regulators have been unable to fully and rigorously examine the universe of such institutions, especially those that decline to participate in the largely voluntary quality assessment programs. More than half of the universities and colleges in India are not funded by the UGC and, thus, are not subject to monitoring according to the standards of its accrediting body, the National Assessment and Accreditation Council (NAAC).[325] In 2006, the NAAC assessed as "medium quality" two-thirds of the Indian colleges subject to its standards, while one-fourth scored "low" and only 9 percent scored "high."[326] Factors contributing to the failure of many Indian institutions to receive high scores include, for example, outdated curricula, limited performance incentives for students and faculty, and limited availability of up-to-date training for faculty.[327] In 2008, faculty vacancy rates reached 50 percent at federal- and state-financed universities,[328] and 20 to 30 percent at

India's most prestigious institutions.[329] Uncompetitive salaries,[330] the limited amount of research conducted at Indian universities relative to that at government-funded research centers, and limited interaction between research centers and universities have contributed to faculty shortages in India.[331]

The Indian government and private investors, such as Anil Agarwal of Vedanta Resources,[332] have endeavored to improve the quality of higher education in India in recent years. Two new UGC regulations entered into force in 2009. One established minimum criteria for awarding Master of Philosophy and Ph.D. degrees and also required that any such degree programs offered through distance education be halted for an indefinite period until assessed for quality. The other strengthened minimum qualifications for faculty appointments and career advancement in universities and affiliated institutions.[333] Also, in response to observations by the Indian Supreme Court, the UGC recently requested that Indian state governments, and state and private universities, take steps to ensure that operations of the universities stay exclusively within the states where they are legally established, and to immediately cease nonconforming operations.[334]

FINANCIAL SERVICES

Overview

The Indian financial services industry is a strong contributor to that nation's economy, accounting for approximately 5.5 percent of GDP in 2007 and creating jobs at a steady pace.[335] There were 939,000 jobs in the Indian banking sector in fiscal year 2009,[336] and according to one industry estimate, that figure had the potential to grow to about 1.2 million by 2010, and to approximately 2.5 million by 2020.[337] India's sustained economic growth has created an expanding middle class with disposable income and increasingly sophisticated financial services needs. Indian households save an average of 32 percent of their income, yet less than half of that money has made its way into the formal financial system.[338] Furthermore, many Indian businesses are rapidly expanding their domestic and foreign operations and need access to financing. While most developed, and many developing, countries have experienced upheaval in their markets as a result of the global financial crisis, India's financial system has not been seriously impacted. This is largely because Indian banks did not have significant exposure to subprime markets, Indian regulators tend to be conservative, and state-owned banks have had their capital augmented by the government when necessary, though the global liquidity shortage that followed the financial crisis did affect Indian banks' lending levels.[339] All of these factors combine to make the Indian banking industry highly attractive to global banks seeking new growth in developing markets. However, the market is not fully open to foreign participation, and foreign firms that do have a domestic presence face a number of hurdles in competing with their Indian counterparts.

Industry Structure

India's banking system was largely closed to the outside world until the mid-1990s, when reforms opened the market to certain kinds of foreign investment and allowed domestic companies to raise money in overseas markets. Foreign banks immediately seized the opportunity to enter what they viewed as an attractive market, but although the number of foreign firms has grown steadily, their overall presence remains relatively small. The Indian banking industry is dominated by a network of state-owned banks, with private domestic and foreign banks holding smaller shares of the market. Twenty-eight state-owned firms[340] held 70 percent of commercial bank assets at the end of March 2008, while private domestic banks accounted for 22 percent of assets and foreign banks held 8 percent.[341] This represents only marginal growth for private banks over 2005 levels, when they held a combined 26 percent of market share (19 percent held by private domestic firms, and 7 percent held by foreign banks versus 74 percent for state-owned banks).[342]

Table 11. Top 10 commercial banks by loan advances, FY 2009

Bank	Loan advances ($ billion)	Market share (%)
State Bank of India	118.0	18.1
ICICI Bank	47.5	7.3
Punjab National Bank	33.6	5.2
Bank of Baroda	31.3	4.8
Bank of India	31.1	4.8
Canara Bank	30.1	4.6
IDBI Bank	22.5	3.5
HDFC Bank	21.5	3.3
Union Bank of India	21.0	3.2
Central Bank of India	18.6	2.9
Other	276.0	42.4
All banks	651.0	

Source: Reserve Bank of India, Database (accessed November 23, 2009).

The country's largest bank is the State Bank of India (SBI), which held 18 percent of market share as measured by loan advances in FY 2009 (table 11).[343] SBI is listed on the Indian stock exchange, but is majority owned by the central bank, the Reserve Bank of India (RBI). RBI is also the majority owner of 8 of the top 10 domestic banks in India, though the second largest bank in India—ICICI—is privately held. State-owned banks maintain the largest presence in consumer markets, accounting for 90 percent of all bank branches in the country.

Foreign banks operating in India have traditionally catered to global firms operating in that country.[344] However, in recent years foreign banks have expanded their offerings and now compete with domestic banks in both the commercial and retail banking spheres. Citigroup (United States) is the largest foreign bank operating in India, with 1.55 percent of total market share, followed by Standard Chartered Bank (United Kingdom), HSBC (United Kingdom), and ABN Amro Bank (Netherlands), with 1.35, 1.21, and 0.82 percent of market share, respectively.[345] While foreign banks face certain restrictions that limit their ability to expand as quickly as their domestic counterparts, they are more likely to introduce new, innovative products to the marketplace and to operate more efficiently, thereby boosting overall competitiveness.

The banking industry is generally concentrated in urban and semi-urban locations, leaving a majority of the poor, rural population underserved. Bank penetration in urban areas exceeds 100 percent, with many metropolitan Indians holding more than one bank account. By comparison, bank penetration stands at just 19 percent[346] in rural areas, where 73 percent of the population resides.[347] Although the number of bank branches has steadily grown in urban India over the past 15 years, expansion into rural regions has remained stagnant and actually declined relative to population growth. Regional cooperative banks and regional rural banks are the predominant providers of financial services in these areas, but they tend to be small, unprofitable, and poorly regulated,[348] with high levels of non-performing loans and too few resources to provide financial services on a large scale.[349]

It is unlikely that the rural population's demand for financial services will be met by traditional banking methods in the near future because the costs of expanding into underserved areas are high, credit risks are elevated, and returns on investment are not assured. In light of these circumstances, many see mobile banking as a potential solution: India has the world's fastest-growing mobile phone market, and a significant portion of that market is in rural areas (see Telecommunication Services). Further, transaction costs for mobile banking are substantially lower than for traditional branch banking, reducing the risk for banks offering such services. Widespread rollout of mobile banking services to traditionally underserved populations could substantially increase banks' retail business and bring many lower-income citizens into the formal economy. However, guidelines for mobile banking issued by the RBI in 2008 limit such transactions to consumers that already have existing bank accounts,[350] so it is unlikely that rural populations will gain meaningful access to mobile banking services in the near term unless the regulations are revised.

Government Policies Affecting the Industry

The RBI is both the country's central bank and the primary regulator of all activities in the banking industry. One of its concerns is ensuring ample credit for domains designated as priority sectors, including agriculture, small- and medium-sized enterprises, and retail trade, among others.[351] The RBI requires both domestic and foreign banks to engage in priority sector lending, with domestic banks devoting 40 percent of loans to priority sectors and an additional 12 percent of available credit to export financing. Though foreign banks are also required to engage in such lending, the thresholds are lower: 32 percent of loans must be made to priority sectors, of which 12 percent must be devoted to export financing and 10 percent to small-scale enterprises.[352] Generally, such a policy is likely to result in inefficient allocation of capital, hampering bank profitability and potentially leading to an increase in non-performing loans. However, the RBI has reportedly made efforts in recent years to expand the scope of priority industries to include more potentially profitable sectors such as the housing industry, and to bring interest rates in line with commercial rates.[353] As such, both domestic and foreign banks surpassed the required targets noted above in 2008, suggesting that some attractive lending opportunities exist within these sectors.

India's Participation in Global Trade

Since opening its financial services market to foreign participation in the mid-1990s, India has become an increasingly attractive market for exporters of financial services, while its domestic banks actively pursue opportunities for growth in overseas markets. In FY 2009, 13 percent ($3.9 billion) of India's miscellaneous services exports were in financial services, while financial services constituted 12 percent ($3 billion) of miscellaneous services imports.[354] While the Indian government does not make available statistics on foreign affiliate transactions, data on outbound FDI—in the form of joint ventures and wholly owned subsidiaries—indicate that financial services comprised a negligible share of such investment in April–June 2009 (0.4 percent) compared to 3 percent during the same period in 2008,[355] likely reflecting the challenging financial conditions in many of the key overseas banking markets. The State Bank of India registered 53 percent growth in its international loan portfolio during FY 2009 by financing Indian businesses that are expanding abroad, expanding its own presence in overseas markets (most recently Singapore), and by courting the business of non resident Indians.[356]

U.S. cross-border trade in financial services with India is relatively small: exports in 2008 totaled just $411 million, or less than 1 percent of total U.S. financial services exports.[357] Imports registered $344 million in 2008, accounting for 2 percent of total U.S. financial services imports,[358] and are most likely concentrated in trade finance and the provision of services to nonresident Indians. While data on affiliate transactions between the United States and India are not available, FDI data suggest that U.S. firms are increasing their presence in the Indian banking market, while Indian firms have a slowly growing presence in the U.S. market. U.S. investment in Indian depository institutions in 2007 amounted to $2.6 billion,[359] a 54 percent increase over the previous year, while investment in non-depository institutions and insurance was $1.7 billion in 2008, 115 percent higher than 2006 levels. By comparison, Indian investment in U.S. depository institutions in 2008 totaled $357 million, a 6 percent increase from 2006.[360]

Policies toward FDI and Cross-border Trade

Foreign banks that wish to enter the Indian market face considerable challenges. While the market is technically open to foreign participation, there are certain conditions that often prevent outside firms from realizing market opportunities. Under Phase I of the Roadmap for the Presence of Foreign Banks Operating in India—a two-phased plan initiated by the RBI in 2005—a foreign bank may enter the Indian market by establishing a branch or a wholly owned subsidiary, or by purchasing a stake in a domestic bank.[361] However, foreign banks are required to submit branch expansion plans annually for approval, and the process is reportedly slow and subject to non-transparent quotas. In 2007, the RBI granted just 19 approvals to foreign bank branches.[362] This puts foreign banks at a distinct disadvantage, as it limits the amount of capital that they can raise domestically through deposits. It also impacts profitability. According to one study, access to retail deposits is the single biggest driver of profitability for retail banks in India.[363] Finally, a single foreign bank may only acquire 5 percent of any domestic private bank, and total foreign ownership by a group of investors acquiring a private domestic bank is capped at 74 percent.

These restrictions generally represent an improvement over India's existing GATS commitments which, among other things, limit foreign banks to establishing only as branches, and do not commit to allowing investment by foreign banks into private Indian banks.[364] Further, the existing commitments limit the number of licenses that may be granted to newly entering or existing foreign banks to five per year. India's Doha Round offer makes improvements which mirror, and in some cases improve, the Road Map. The offer includes establishment as a wholly owned subsidiary, increases the investment cap by an individual foreign firm in a private Indian bank to 49 percent, and raises the number of licenses granted to foreign banks to 20 annually.[365]

Phase II of the roadmap, which was scheduled for implementation in April 2009, would ease foreign firms' access to the market by allowing mergers and acquisitions with private domestic banks, accord full national treatment to wholly owned subsidiaries of foreign banks, and require wholly owned subsidiaries to divest 26 percent of stock to resident Indians, either as a direct sale or through an initial public offering. However, the RBI has postponed implementation, citing uncertainties resulting from the global financial crisis.[366] The RBI has not indicated when it will move forward with the new measures.

TOPICS FOR FURTHER ANALYSIS

This study has provided an overview of the service sector in India and has examined six service industries in detail. Future studies might examine prominent service industries not analyzed in this report. For example, while distribution services (wholesale and retail trade) account for the largest share of services output and employment in India, the Indian government heavily restricts foreign participation in the retail industry. Leading multinational retailers, such as Wal-Mart and Tesco, have sought to enter the retail market indirectly by establishing wholesale businesses that sell merchandise to Indian retailers. However, the Indian government has taken steps to limit this practice.[367] Further research is needed on the motivations for the restrictions and on the potential effects of liberalization on the Indian retail industry and the economy. Other major sectors that merit deeper investigation include logistic services and travel services—both prominent in U.S.-India services trade (figures 3 and 4)—and professional services such as law, accounting, and healthcare, all of which are subject to market access limitations.[368]

Future analyses could also investigate more broadly the potential effects of greater liberalization. This paper examined possible impacts on service imports into India; it would also be useful to explore effects on India's goods imports, goods and services exports, output, employment, and poverty.[369] Finally, the Indian experience with service sector development might be compared with that of other key emerging economies, including Brazil, China, Indonesia, Mexico, Russia, and Vietnam.

APPENDIX

Table A.1. 2000–06 summary statistics

Variable	Observations	Mean	Standard Deviation	Minimum	Maximum
ln (Services Imports)	4582	4.54	2.53	-4.91	10.66
ln (Importer's GDP)	4554	25.92	1.47	22.45	29.26
ln (Exporter's GDP)	4682	26.34	1.36	23.73	30.05
ln (Distance)	4682	8.15	1.12	4.09	9.87
ln (Importer's Remoteness)	4682	-12.60	0.91	-13.86	-10.98
ln (Exporter's Remoteness)	4682	-12.07	1.38	-15.99	-9.77
Adjacency	4682	0.07	0.25	0	1
Common Language	4682	0.08	0.27	0	1
Services FDI Restrictiveness	4682	0.24	0.14	0.04	0.67

Table A.2. 2004 summary statistics

Variable	Observations	Mean	Standard Deviation	Minimum	Maximum
ln (services imports)	881	4.72	2.43	-4.39	10.49
ln (importer's GDP)	873	25.92	1.45	22.74	29.22
ln (exporter's GDP)	897	26.28	1.31	23.87	29.99
ln (distance)	897	8.13	1.12	4.09	9.87
ln (importer's remoteness)	897	-14.29	0.92	-15.56	-12.56
ln (exporter's remoteness)	897	-12.33	0.59	-20.11	-11.83
Adjacency	897	0.07	0.25	0	1
Common language	897	0.08	0.27	0	1
Services FDI Restrictiveness	897	0.24	0.14	0.04	0.67

Table A.3. 2000–06 correlation matrix

	$\ln Y_i$	$\ln Y_j$	$\ln D_{ij}$	$\ln REM_i$	$\ln REM_j$	A_{ij}	CL_{ij}	$SFDIR_{ij}$
$\ln Y_i$	1.00							
$\ln Y_j$	0.10	1.00						
$\ln D_{ij}$	0.20	0.14	1.00					
$\ln REM_i$	0.29	0.07	0.79	1.00				
$\ln REM_j$	-0.12	-0.97	-0.09	-0.07	1.00			
A_{ij}	0.07	0.03	-0.44	-0.19	-0.06	1.00		
CL_{ij}	0.05	0.10	0.04	0.10	-0.07	0.18	1.00	
$SFDIR_{ij}$	0.05	0.03	0.44	0.56	-0.02	-0.11	0.06	1.00

Table A.4. 2004 correlation matrix

	$\ln Y_i$	$\ln Y_j$	$\ln D_{ij}$	$\ln REM_i$	$\ln REM_j$	A_{ij}	CL_{ij}	$SFDIR_{ij}$
$\ln Y_i$	1.00							
$\ln Y_j$	0.09	1.00						
$\ln D_{ij}$	0.21	0.14	1.00					
$\ln REM_i$	0.26	0.06	0.81	1.00				
$\ln REM_j$	-0.18	-0.39	-0.06	-0.06	1.00			
A_{ij}	0.06	0.03	-0.44	-0.21	-0.10	1.00		
CL_{ij}	0.06	0.09	0.03	0.09	-0.06	0.19	1.00	
$SFDIR_{ij}$	0.07	0.04	0.46	0.56	-0.02	-0.12	0.06	1.00

BIBLIOGRAPHY

Air India. Management Discussion and Analysis Report. *Annual Report 2006–2007*. New Delhi: Air India, n.d. http://home.airindia.in/SBCMS/downloads/ManagementDiscussion&AnalysisReport 0607.pdf.

Agarwal, Pawan. "Higher Education in India: The Need for Change." Indian Council for Research on International Economic Relations (ICRIER). Working Paper no. 180, June 2006. http://www.icrier.org/pdf/icrier wp180 Higher Education in India.pdf.

Ahluwalia, Montek. "Economic Reforms in India Since 1991: Has Gradualism Worked?" *Journal of Economic Perspectives* 16, no. 3 (2002): 67–88.

Ahmed, Sadiq, and Ejaz Ghani. "South Asia's Growth and Regional Integration: An Overview." In *South Asia: Growth and Regional Integration*, edited by Sadiq Ahmed and Ejaz Ghani. New Delhi: Macmillan India, 2007. http://siteresources.worldbank.org/SOUTH ASIAEXT/Resources/Publications/448813-171648504958/SouthAsia GrowthandRegionalIntegration.pdf.

Anderson, James E., and Eric Van Wincoop. "Gravity with Gravitas: A Solution to the Border Puzzle." *American Economic Review* 93, no. 1 (March 2003): 170 – 92.

Anitha, B.K., and Bhushan Patwardhan. "Emerging Directions in Global Education." *Current Science* 95, no. 3 (August 10, 2008): 303–04. http://www.ias.ac.in/currsci/aug102008/303.pdf.

ArabianBusiness.com. "India Ministry Plans Cargo Airports," April 1, 2007. http://www.arabianbusiness.com/ (accessed October 16, 2009).

A.T. Kearney. *The Shifting Geography of Offshoring: The 2009 A.T. Kearney Global Services Location Index*. Chicago: A.T. Kearney, 2009. http://www.atkearney.com/index.php/Publications/globalservices-location-index-gsli-2009-report.html.

Baier, Scott L., and Jeffrey H. Bergstrand. "*Bonus Vetus* OLS: A Simple Method for Approximating International Trade-cost Effects Using the Gravity Equation." *Journal of International Economics* 77, no. 1 (2009): 77 – 85.

Baker, Peter. "Senate Approves Indian Nuclear Deal." *New York Times*, October 1, 2008. http://www.nytimes.com/2008/10/02/washington/02webnuke.html?scp=1&sq=us%20india%20nu clear%20deal&st=cse.

Banga, Rashmi. "Critical Issues in India's Service-Led Growth." Indian Council for Research on International Economic Relations (ICRIER). Working Paper no. 171, October 2005.

Belgaonkar, Anubhuti, and Krishna Chinta. *India (Country Regulation and Overview)*. London: Ovum, April 15, 2009.

Bhuyan, Rituparna. "Saarc Meet to Fast-track Services Trade, Expand Safta Regulation." *Financial Express*, October 29, 2009.

Bisignani, Giovanni. "Confederation of Indian Industry—Remarks of Giovanni Bisignani." Speech delivered at the Confederation of Indian Industry, Delhi, September 24, 2008. http://www.iata.org/pressroom/speeches/Pages/2008-09-24-01.aspx (accessed June 4, 2010).

Blonigen, Bruce A. "In Search of Substitution between Foreign Production and Exports." *Journal of International Economics* 53, no.1 (February 2001): 81–104.

Bureau van Dijk. Orbis database. https://orbis.bvdep.com (accessed various dates).

Business Monitor International (BMI). *India Telecommunications Report Q4 2009*. London: BMI, September 2009.

Case Studies and Management Resources. "Kingfisher Airlines Acquires a Stake in Air Deccan: The Indian Aviation Sector Moves towards Consolidation," August 22, 2007. http://www.icmrindia.org/ (accessed September 28, 2009).

Cathers, Dylan. *Industry Surveys: Computers; Commercial Services*. New York: Standard & Poor's, May 2009. http://www.netadvantage.standardandpoors.com/ (subscription required).

Centres D'Etudes Prospectives et D'Information, Global Distances database. http://www.cepii.fr/anglaisgraph/bdd/distances.htm (accessed October 17, 2009).

Chadha, Rajesh, Drusilla Brown, Alan Deardorff, and Robert Stern. "Computational Analysis of the Impact on India of the Uruguay Round and the Doha Development Agenda Negotiations." In *India and the WTO*, edited by Aaditya Mattoo and Robert Stern, 13–46. Washington DC: World Bank and Oxford University Press, 2003.

Chadwick, William, Jr. "Global Trends in the Information Technology Outsourcing Services Market." *Industry Trade and Technology Review*, USITC publication no. 3661 (November 2003): 1–9.

Cheney, Gretchen Rhines, Betsy Brown Ruzzi, and Karthik Muralidharan. "A Profile of the Indian Education System." Prepared for the New Commission on the Skills of the American Workforce, November 2005. http://www.skillscommission.org/study.htm.

Council of Graduate Schools (CGS). *Findings from the 2009 CGS International Graduate Admissions Survey: Phase III; Final Offers of*

Admission and Enrollment. Washington, DC: Council of Graduate Schools, November 2009. http://www.cgsnet.org/portals/0/pdf/R intlenr l09 III.pdf.

CSO. *See* Government of India, Ministry of Statistics and Programme Implementation, Central Statistical Organisation.

De Mel, Deshal. "India–Sri Lanka: Comprehensive Economic Partnership Agreement." *World Trade Net*, October 15, 2008. http://www. economicswebinstitute. org/essays/cepaindiasrilanka.pdf.

Dharmakumar, Rhohin, and Shishir Prasad. "Bharti Minutes in Africa." *Forbes.com*, April 28, 2010. http://www.forbes.com/2010/04/27/forbes-india-bharti-minutes-factory-goes-to-africa.html.

Directorate General of Civil Aviation. "Airline-wise Financial Status of All Scheduled Indian Carriers (2001–2002 to 2003–2004 and 2006–2007)," n.d. http://www.indiastat.com/table/transport/30/civilaviation/ 62/281436/ data.aspx (accessed September 14, 2009; subscription required).

———. "Category-wise Personnel Statistics of Scheduled Indian Carriers (1999–2000 to 2006–2007)," n.d. http://www.indiastat.com/table/transport /30/civilaviation/62/70126/data.aspx (accessed September 14, 2009; subscription required).

———. "Domestic Passengers Carried by Air India and Private Airlines in India (2005 to 2008)," n.d. http://www.indiastat.com/table/transport civilaviation/62/453209/data.aspx (accessed September 14, 2009; subscription required).

———. "Financial Results of Scheduled Domestic Private Airlines of India (2007–2008)," n.d. http://www.indiastat.com/Transport/30/CivilAviation/62/460448/data.asp x (accessed September 14, 2009; subscription required).

Directorate General of Civil Aviation. Statistical Division. *India Air Transport Statistics, 2007–08.* New Delhi: Directorate General of Civil Aviation, April 2009. http://dgca.gov.in/reports/stat-ind.htm.

Doig, Stephen, Ronald Ritter, Kurt Speckhals, and Daniel Woolson. "Has Outsourcing Gone Too Far?" *McKinsey Quarterly* 4 (2001): 25–37.

Dongaonkar, Dayanand, and Usha Rai Negi. *International Students in Indian Universities, 2007–2008.* New Delhi, India: Association of Indian Universities, 2009. http://www.aiuweb.org/research/isiu2009.doc.

Dow Jones Newswires. "MTNL Eyes African Market," January 20, 2010. http://www.totaltele.com/view.aspx?ID452235&mail=177&C=5 (subscription required).

Dun & Bradstreet. "India's Top IT Companies 2008," February 2008. http://www.dnb.co.in/TopIT 08/default.asp.

Economist. "Bittersweet Synergy," October 22, 2009. http://www.economist. com/node/14710627 (registration required).

———. "Clash of the Clouds," October 15, 2009. http://www.economist.com /node/14637206 (registration required).

———. "Flight to Value," August 8, 2009. http://www.economist.com /node/14179187 (registration required).

———. "Not Entirely Free, Your Honour," July 31, 2010.

———. "Ruled by Lakshmi," December 13, 2008. http://www. economist. com/node/12749719 (registration required).

———. "Storm-clouds Gathering," December 11, 2008. http://www.economist.com/node/12749795 (registration required).

Economist Intelligence Unit (EIU). *Country Profile: India*. London: Economist Intelligence Unit, 2008.

———. *Country Finance: India*. New York: Economist Intelligence Unit, July 2009.

———. "India Alternatives: Great Leap Forward." *ViewsWire*, May 5, 2009.

———. "India Coal: Opening Up." *ViewsWire*, June 12, 2009.

———. "India Energy: Piecemeal Reforms." *ViewsWire*, June 1, 2009.

———. "India: Energy Report." *ViewsWire*, May 26, 2009.

Evans, Peter. *India: Telecoms, Mobile, and Broadband, and Forecasts*. Bucketty, Australia: Paul Budde Communication Pty Ltd, June 2009.

Farrell, Diana, and Eric Beinhocker. "Next Big Spenders: India's Middle Class." *BusinessWeek*, May 19, 2007. http://www.mckinsey.com /mgi/ mginews /bigspenders.asp.

Fernandez, Enric, and Poonam Gupta. "Understanding the Growth Momentum in India's Services." *India Goes Global: Its Expanding Role in the World Economy*. Washington, DC: International Monetary Fund, 2006.

Gartner. "Gartner Says Worldwide IT Services Revenue Grew 8.2 Percent in 2008." Press release, June 9, 2009. http://www.gartner.com/it/page.jsp?id =1011512.

Gera, Komal Amit. "IT Players Concerned over Extension of STPI Act." *Business Standard,* March 12, 2010. http://www.business-standard.com/india/printpage.php?autono=388296&tp.

Ghani, Ejaz, and Homi Kharas. "The Service Revolution." World Bank Poverty Reduction and Economic Management Network (PREM). Economic Premise 14, May 2010.

Gilmore, Agatha, Mike Prokopeak, Kellye Whitney, Deanna Hartley, Lindsay Edmonds Wickman, and Brian Summerfield. "Salary Survey 2008." *Certification,* December 2008. http://www.certmag.com/read.php? start= 0&in=3656.

Gordon, James, and Poonam Gupta. "Understanding India's Services Revolution." IMF Working Paper 04/171, September 2004.

Gohain, K. "Airline Operations Regulatory Issues in India." PowerPoint presentation, n.d. http://civilaviation.nic.in/jdg pres.ppt (accessed October 5, 2009).

Golub, Stephen S. "Openness to Foreign Direct Investment in Services: An International Comparative Analysis." *The World Economy* 32, no. 8 (2009): 1245 – 68.

Government of India. Labour Bureau. "Statistics: Occupational Wage Surveys." n.d. http://labourbureau.nic.in/OWS%20New%20Table.htm (accessed July 27, 2009).

Government of India. Ministry of Civil Aviation. *Annual Report, 2008–09.* New Delhi: Ministry of Civil Aviation, September 2009. http://www.civilaviation.nic.in/annualReports.htm.

Government of India. Ministry of Finance. "Civil Aviation." *Economic Survey 2008–09.* New Delhi: Ministry of Finance, 2009. http://indiabudget.nic.in (accessed September 15, 2009).

Government of India. Ministry of Human Resource Development. *Annual Report 2007–08.* New Delhi: Ministry of Human Resources Development, 2008. http://www.education.nic.in/AR/annualreports.asp (accessed June 8, 2010).

Government of India. Ministry of Human Resource Development. Department of Higher Education. "New Policy on Distance Learning in Higher Education Sector." Public Notice F.no.6-9/2009- DL, August 28, 2009. http://www.education.nic.in/dl/dl-new.asp.

Government of India. Ministry of Statistics and Programme Implementation. Central Statistical Organisation. *National Accounts Statistics: Sources and Methods, 2007.* New Delhi: Central Statistical Organisation, March 2007. http://mospi.gov.in/manual_compilation.htm/.

———. *National Accounts Statistics, 2006–07.* New Delhi: Central Statistical Organisation, May 2009. http://www.mospi.nic.in/.

———. *Statistical Abstract of India 2007.* "Table 19.1—Indian Scheduled Operations." New Delhi: Central Statistical Organisation, 2008.

Government of India. Ministry of Trade and Industry. Department of Commerce. "Trade Agreements." http://commerce.nic.in/trade/ international ta.asp?id=2&trade=i (accessed October 19, 2009).

———. "Trade in Services: Requests to Developed Countries; USA," n.d. http://commerce.nic.in/trade/international trade tis gaitis requests rtc rtdc1.asp (accessed October 19, 2009).

Government of India. Planning Commission. *Eleventh Five-Year Plan 2007– 2012.* Vol. 1, *Inclusive Growth.* New Delhi: Oxford University Press, 2008. http://planningcommission.gov.in/plans/planrel/fiveyr/welcome.html.

———. *Integrated Energy Policy: Report of the Expert Committee.* New Delhi: Planning Commission, August 2006. http://planningcommission.gov.in/reports/genrep/rep_intengy.pdf.

Grünfeld, Leo A., and Andreas Moxnes. "The Intangible Globalization: Explaining the Patterns of International Trade in Services." Norwegian Institute of International Affairs. Working Paper 657, 2003.

Guha, Romit, R. Jai Krishna, and Kenanj Machado. "India's Wireless Broadband Auction Ends." *Dow Jones Newswires,* June 11, 2010. http://www.totaltele.com/printablearticle.aspx?ID=456277 (subscription required).

Gupta, Amit. *Trends in 2010: India Telecoms Market.* London: Ovum, February 3, 2010.

Gupta, Asha. "Caste, Class, and Quality at the Indian Institutes of Technology." *International Higher Education* 53 (Fall 2008). http://www.bc.edu/bc   org/avp/soe/cihe/newsletter/Number53/p20 Gupta.htm.

Heath, Nick. "Mahindra Satyam Boss Talks Up Prospects." *Bloomberg Businessweek,* August 11, 2009. http://www.businessweek.com /globalbiz/content /aug2009/gb20090811 178412.htm.

Helpman, Elhanan, Marc J. Melitz, and Stephen R. Yeaple. "Export versus FDI." National Bureau of Economic Research. Working Paper 9439, January 2003.

Heng, Ek. "SingTel Increases Stake in India's Bharti Airtel." *Telecommunications Online*, November 2, 2009. http://telecomengine. com/Print.asp?Id=AR_5861.

Herbst, Moira. "Indian Firms, Microsoft Top H-1B List." *BusinessWeek*, February 24, 2009.

Hindu. "Jet Acquires Air Sahara Finally," April 13, 2007. http://www. hindu.com/2007/04/13/stories/2007041302151300.htm.

Holman, David, Rosemary Batt, and Ursula Holtgrewe. *The Global Call Center Report: International Perspectives on Management and Employment; Report of the Global Call Center Network.* Ithaca, NY: ILR School, Cornell University, 2007.

Hooper, Paul. "Liberalisation of the Airline Industry in India." *Journal of Transportation Management* 3, no. 3 (1997), 116–17.

Hot Telecom. *Country Profile: India.* Montreal, Canada: Hot Telecom, July 2009.

IBA Newswatch. "India's Budget Airlines Leave Rivals in Vapour Stream." Volume 9, no. 35 (September 11, 2009): 8.

IBM. "IBM Opens Four Cloud Computing Centers to Meet Growing Demand in Emerging Markets." Press release, September 24, 2008. http://www-03.ibm.com/press/us/en/pressrelease/25196.wss#feeds.

IndiaStat. "Employed Workers in Selected Industrys *[sic]* in India (1993–1994, 1999–2000 and 2004–2005)." Compiled from the statistics released by Lok Sabha, Unstarred Question no. 1208, November 26, 2001, and Lok Sabha, Unstarred Question no. 4009, April 21, 2008. http://www.indiastat.com/table/labourandworkforce/380987/employmentinindustries/18527/21415/data.aspx (accessed August 3, 2009; subscription required).

———."Growth of IT-ITES Professionals in India (1999–2000 to 2005–2006)." Compiled from statistics released by the Ministry of Communications and Information Technology, Government of India. http://www.indiastat.com/table/labourandworkforce/380987/employmentinindustries/18527/446460/data.aspx. (accessed August 3, 2009; subscription required).

———. "Profit and Loss of Selected Airlines of India (2005–2006 to 2007–2008)." Compiled using data from Rajya Sabha Unstarred Question No. 137, February 17, 2009. http://www.indiastat.com/Transport/30/CivilAviation/62/458148/data.aspx (accessed September 14, 2009; subscription required).

———. "Growth of Student Enrolment in Universities and Colleges of India (1979–1980 to 2004– 2005)." Compiled using data from the Ministry of Human Resource Development, Government of India. http://www.indiastat.com/table/education/6370/enrolmentinhighereducationclassesabovexii/3668 01/13438/data.aspx (accessed September 1, 2009; subscription required).

———. "Region/Country-wise Enrolment of Foreign Students in Indian Universities (2001–2002 to 2004–2005)." Compiled from the statistics released by Lok Sabha, Unstarred Question no. 40, dated March 1, 2005, and Lok Sabha, Unstarred Question no. 4130, dated April 22, 2008. http://www.indiastat.com/table/education/6370/ enrolmentinhighereducationclassesabovexii/3668   01/355663/data.aspx (accessed September 1, 2009; subscription required).

————. State-wise Number of Higher Educational Institutions in India (2006–2007). Compiled using data from the Ministry of Human Resource Development, Government of India. http://www.indiastat.com/Education /6370/UniversitiesCollegesInstitutionsforHigherEducation/36 9742/459837/data.aspx (accessed September 1, 2009; subscription required).

Indira Gandhi National Open University (IGNOU). "IGNOU Profile 2008," 2008. http://www.ignou.ac.in/ (accessed September 28, 2009).

Ionides, Nicholas. "India Unleashed." *Airline Business* 22, no. 7 (July 2006): 35–37.

International Air Transport Association (IATA). "Passenger and Freight Forecasts 2007 to 2011." *IATA Economic Briefing*, October 2007. http://iata.org/economics(accessed October 14, 2009).

International Monetary Fund (IMF). "Balance of Payments Statistics: Classification and Standard Components of the Balance of Payments," September 4, 2007. http://www.imfstatistics.org/imf/BOPClass.htm.

International Telecommunication Union. *ITU World Telecommunication/ICT Indicators 2009* (accessed May 12, 2010).

Jog, Sanjay. "NTPC to Follow National Tariff Policy, Buy Power Competitively from 2011." *Financial Express*, August 20, 2009. http://www.financialexpress.com/news/ntpc-to-follownational-tariff-policy-buy-power-competitively-from-2011/504049/.

Kanth, Ravi. "Revised Text Needed for Doha Round Success: India." *Rediff*, May 8, 2008. http://www.rediff.com/money/2008/may/08wto.htm.

Kapur, Devesh, and Ravi Ramamurti. "India's Emerging Competitive Advantage in Services." *Academy of Management Executive* 15, no. 2, 2001, 20–33.

Kapur, Devesh, and Megan Crowley. "Beyond the ABCs: Higher Education and Developing Countries." Center for Global Development. Working Paper no. 139, February 2008. http://www.cgdev.org/ publications /content/15310.

Kapur, Devesh, and Pratap Bhanu Mehta. "Mortgaging the Future? Indian Higher Education." Paper prepared for the Brookings-NCAER India

Policy Forum 2007–08, December 26, 2007. http://casi.ssc.upenn.edu /about/people/devesh/.

Kimura, Fukunari, and Hyun-Hoon Lee. "The Gravity Equation in International Trade in Services." *Review of World Economics* 142, no. 1 (April 2006): 92 – 121.

Krishna, R. Jai. "BSNL Looking to Buy Small Companies Abroad." *Dow Jones Newswires*, December 3, 2009. http://www.totaltele.com/ view.aspx?ID=451249&mail=150&C=5 (subscription required).

———. "India's TRAI Asks Govt Not to Issue New Licenses." *Dow Jones Newswires*, August 5, 2009. http://www.totaltele.com/printablearticle. aspx?ID=447896 (subscription required).

Krishna, R. Jai, and Romit Guha. "BSNL, MTNL Have Cash to Meet 3G Bandwidth Fees." *Dow Jones Newswires*, May 20, 2010. http://www.totaltele.com/printablearticle.aspx?ID=45584 (subscription required).

Krishna, R. Jai, Romit Guha, and Nikhil Gulati. "Indian Regulator Recommends Easing Merger Rules." *Dow Jones Newswires*, May 11, 2010. http://www.totaltele.com/printablearticle.aspx?ID=455376 (sub-scription required).

Lakshman, Nandini. "India to Foreign Colleges: Set Up Campus Here." *Time*, July 31, 2009. http://www.time.com/time/world/article/0,8599,1913653, 00.html.

Lamont, James. "India Lashes Out at US Visa Regime." *Financial Times,* August 10, 2010.http://www.ft.com/cms/s/0/5a186610-a487-11df-abf7-00144feabdc0.html.

Leahy, Joe. "Bharti Seals Deal for Zain Networks." *Financial Times*, March 30, 2010.

http://www.ft.com/cms/s/0/993a137e-3c28-11df-b40c-00144feabdc0.html (subscription required).

———. "A Tough Call." *Financial Times*. May 25, 2010. http://www.ft.com/cms/s/0/64dde3b4-6796-11df-a932-00144feab49a.html (subscription required).

Lennighan, Mary. "Friday Review: Into India." *Total Telecom*, September 25, 2009. http://www.totaltele.com/view.aspx?ID=449278.

Leung, Rebecca. "Out of India: More American Companies Are Sending Jobs Overseas." *60 Minutes,* August 1, 2004. http://www.cbsnews.com/ (accessed August 27, 2009).

Levy, Daniel. "Access through Private Higher Education: Global Patterns and Indian Illustrations." University of Albany. Program for Research on

Private Higher Education. Working Paper no. 11, April 2008. http://www.albany.edu/dept/eaps/prophe/publication/paper.html#WP11.

———. "Indian Private Higher Education in Comparative Perspective." University of Albany. Program for Research on Private Higher Education. Working Paper no. 13, October 2008. http://www.albany.edu/dept/eaps/prophe/publication/paper.html#WP13.

Mamta. "Mobiles Can Build a More Inclusive Financial System." *Indian Council for Research on International Economic Relations (ICRIER) Think Ink*, June 1, 2009. http://www.icrier.org/page.asp? MenuID =24&SubCatId=177 (accessed June 8, 2010).

Mattoo, Aaditya, Deepak Mishra, and Anirudh Shingal. *Sustaining India's Services Revolution: Access to Foreign Markets, Domestic Reform, and International Negotiations*. New Delhi: World Bank, 2004.http://web.worldbank.org/WBSITE/EXTERNAL/COUNTRIES/SO UTHASIAEXT/EXTSARRE GTOPINT ECOTRA/0, contentMDK: 20855381~ page PK:34004173~piPK:34003707~theSitePK: 579448, 00. html.

Mattoo, Aaditya, and Arvind Subramanian. "India and the Multilateral Trading System Post-Doha: Defensive or Proactive?" In *India and the WTO*, edited by Aaditya Mattoo and Robert Stern, 327–66. Washington DC: World Bank and Oxford University Press, 2003.

McKinsey & Company. *India: The Growth Imperative*. McKinsey Global Institute, September 2001. http://www.mckinsey.com/mgi/ publications/ india.asp (subscription required).

———. *Indian Banking: Towards Global Best Practices; Insights from Industry Benchmarking Surveys*. McKinsey & Company, November 2007. http://www.mckinsey.com/locations/india/mckinseyonindia/pdf/India Banking Overview.pdf.

McKinsey & Company and NASSCOM. *NASSCOM-McKinsey Report 2005: Extending India's Leadership of the Global IT and BPO Industries*. New Delhi: NASSCOM, 2005. http://www.mckinsey.com/locations/india/ mckinseyonindia/pdf/NASSCOM_McKinsey_Report_ 2005.pdf.

———. *Perspective 2020: Transform Business, Transform India*. New Delhi: NASSCOM, April 2009.

Mehrotra, Santosh. "Indian Higher Education: Time for a Serious Rethink." *International Higher Education* 56 (Summer 2009). http://www.bc.edu/bc org/avp/soe/cihe/newsletter/Number56/p5 Mehrotra. htm.

Middleton, James. "India's Bharti Moves into Bangladesh." *Telecoms.com*, January 12, 2010. http://www.telecoms.com/17364/india%e2%80%99s-bharti-moves-into-bangladesh.

———. "India's 3G Licensing Auction Finally Over." *Telecoms.com*, May 20, 2010. http://www.telecoms.com/20433/india%E2%80%99s-3g-licensing-auction-finally-over/.

Molnar, Margit, Nigel Pain, and Daria Taglioni. "Globalisation and Employment in the OECD." *OECD Economic Studies,* no. 44 (2008): 1–34.

Monger, Randall, and Macreadie Barr. "Nonimmigrant Admissions to the United States: 2008." *2008 Yearbook of Immigration Statistics*. Washington, DC: Department of Homeland Security, April 2009. http://www.dhs.gov/xlibrary/assets/statistics/publications/ois   ni   fr 2008.pdf.

Mukherjee, Arpita, and Ramneet Goswami. "Trade in Energy Services: GATS and India." Indian Council for Research on International Economic Relations (ICRIER). Working Paper no. 231, January 2009.

Narayanan, Arun. "India Poised for Air Cargo Revolution." *Air Cargo World*, September 2009. http://www.aircargoworld.com/ (accessed September 17, 2009).

NASSCOM. *The IT-BPO Sector in India: Strategic Review 2009*. New Delhi: NASSCOM, February 2009.

———. *The IT-BPO Sector in India: Strategic Review 2010*. New Delhi: NASSCOM, February 2010. http://www.nasscom.in/upload/SR10/ExecutiveSummary.pdf (Executive summary available for free; fee required for full report).

Nayyar, Deepak. "The Internationalization of Firms from India: Investment, Mergers and Acquisitions." *Oxford Development Studies* 36, no. 1 (March 2008): 111–31.

Neelakantan, Shailaja. "India Struggles to Become a Destination for Foreign Students." *Chronicle of Higher Education*, July 10, 2009.

———. "India's Faculty Shortage Hits Elite Business Schools." *Chronicle of Higher Education*, December 12, 2008. http://chronicle.com/article/Indias-Faculty-Shortage-Hits/42112/.

———. "Rapid Expansion Strains Elite Indian Institutes." *Chronicle of Higher Education*, January 30, 2009.

Oanda. Historical Exchange Rates database. http://www.oanda.com/currency/historical-rates (accessed August 17, 2010).

O'Connell, John F., and George Williams. "Transformation of India's Domestic Airlines: A Case Study of Indian Airlines, Jet Airways, Air Sahara and Air Deccan." *Journal of Air Transport Management* 12 (2006): 359–63.

Office of the United States Trade Representative (USTR). "India." *2009 National Trade Estimate Report on Foreign Trade Barriers*. Washington, DC: USTR, 2009.

———. "United States and India Sign Framework for Cooperation on Trade and Investment." Press release, March 17, 2010. http://www.ustr.gov/about-us/press-office/pressreleases/2010/march/united-states-and-india-sign-framework-cooperation-t.

Organisation for Economic Co-operation and Development (OECD). "Economic Survey of India, 2007."OECD Policy Brief, October 2007. http://www.oecd.org/dataoe cd/17/52/39452196.pdf.

———. *OECD Economic Surveys: India*. Paris: OECD, October 2007.

OECD. OECD.Stat Extracts: Trade in Services by Partner Country database. http://stats.oecd.org/index.aspx?r=170404 (accessed various dates).

———. *OECD Statistics on International Trade in Services, 1970–2006*. Paris: OECD, 2008. Accessed via SourceOECD. http://puck.sourceoecd.org/vl=1902441/cl=11/nw=1/rpsv/home.htm (subscription required) (accessed September 29, 2009).

Pan, Esther, and Jayshree Bajoria. "The U.S.-India Nuclear Deal." New York: Council on Foreign Relations, October 2, 2008. http://www.cfr.org/publication/9663/.

Patnaik, Nageshwar. "Orissa Passes Vedanta University Bill with Amendments." *Economic Times*, July 30, 2009._http://economictimes.indiatimes.com/articleshow/4838857.cms.

PayScale. Salary Snapshot database. http://www.payscale.com/research/IN/Job=Software_Engineer_%2F_Developer_%2F_Program mer/Salary and http://www.payscale.com/research/US/Job=Software Engineer %2F Developer %2F Program mer/Salary (accessed August 3, 2010).

People's Daily Online. "Indian Civil Aviation Giant Jet Airways Acquires Air Sahara," January 20, 2006. http://english.peopledaily.com.cn/.

Pereira, John. "India: Not Just Another BRIC in the Wall." *Money Management*, January 29, 2009, 20.

Poddar, Tushar, and Eva Yi. "India's Rising Growth Potential." Goldman Sachs Global Economics Paper no. 152, January 22, 2007. http://www.usindiafriendship.net/viewpoints1/Indias Rising Growth Potential.pdf.

Ramanathan, Gayatri. "AES Lines Up Largest Investment in Power." *LiveMint*, June 18, 2007.

Reserve Bank of India (RBI). "Annual Policy Statement—2009–10." Press release, April 21, 2009. http://rbidocs.rbi.org.in/rdocs/PressRelease/PDFs/EPR1736APS09.pdf.

———. "A Profile of Banks 2008–09." Mumbai: Reserve Bank of India, September 9, 2009. http://rbi.org.in/scripts/ AnnualPublications.aspx?head=A%20Profile%20of%20Banks.

———. Database. http://www.rbi.org.in/scripts/statistics.aspx (accessed various dates).

———. "India's Balance of Payments Developments during the First Quarter (April–June 2009) of 2009–2010." *RBI Monthly Bulletin*, October 2009. http://www.rbi.org.in/scripts/BS/ViewBulletin.aspx.

———. "Indian Investment Abroad in Joint Ventures and Wholly Owned Subsidiaries: 2009–10 (April– June)." *RBI Monthly Bulletin*, October 2009. http://www.rbi.org.in/scripts/ BS_ViewBulletin.aspx.

———. "Mobile Banking Transaction in India–Operative Guidelines for Banks." RBI/2008–09/208, October 8, 2008. http://rbidocs.rbi.org.in/rdocs/notification/PDFs/87664.pdf.

———. *RBI Monthly Bulletin,* July 2009. http://www.rbi.org.in/scripts /BS_ViewBulletin.aspx.

———. *Reserve Bank of India Annual Report 2008–09.* Mumbai: Reserve Bank of India, August 27, 2009. http://www.rbi.org.in/scripts /AnnualReportPublications.aspx.

———. "Roadmap for the Presence of Foreign Banks Operating in India," February 28, 2005. http://www.rbi.org.in/upload/content/images /RoadMap.html.

Reuters. "India Working on MVNO Guidelines—Telecom Secy," June 25, 2010. http://www.reuters.com/article/idUKBMA00790520100625.

Reuters. "Talent Building Key Challenge for India." *Indianexpress.com*, August 11, 2009. http://www.indianexpress.com/story-print/500660/ (accessed August 12, 2009).

Ribeiro, John. "India Delays Mobile Number Portability Again." *Bloomberg Businessweek*, July 7, 2010. http://www.businessweek.com/idg/2010-07-01/india-delays-mobile-number-portabilityagain.html.

Roy, Arup, Kamlesh Bhatia, Jim Longwood, and King-Yew Foong. "Wipro Infotech Wins IT Outsourcing Deal With Aircel." Gartner RAS Core Research Note G00156017, April 1, 2008. http://www.wipro.in /newsroom/wiprointhenews/NC AircelGartner.pdf.

Roy, Saumya. "A Backdoor That Leads Nowhere." *Forbes India*, May 10, 2010. http://www.forbes.com/2010/05/10/forbes-india-a-backdoor-that-leads-nowhere.html.

Saadi, Dania. "Batelco Begins Telecom Operations in India." *Dow Jones Newswires*, December 16, 2009. http://www.totaltele.com /view.aspx? ID45163&mail=159&C=1 (subscription required).

Sahasrabudhe, Ujjaini, and Swetha Muthanna. "Making Sense of Accreditation for Higher Education Institutions in India." Conference presentation at NAFSA: Association of International Educators, Los Angeles, CA, May 2009. http://www.ierf.org/publicationsarticles.asp.

Sanders, Lee. "The German and India Spectrum Auctions: Did Operators Get Value for Money?" *Analysys Mason [sic]*, May 14, 2010. http://www.analysysmason.com.

Scully, Vaughan. *Global Industry Surveys: Electric Utilities; Asia*. New York: Standard & Poor's, April 2007. www.netadvantage.standardandpoors.com (subscription required).

Sen, Amiti. "India Seeks Demand List from Asean Nations." *Economic Times*, December 14, 2009. http://economictimes.indiatimes.com/news/economy/ foreign-trade/India-seeks-demand-list-fromAsean-nations/articleshow/5334705.cms.

Seshagiri, Mathang. "All Seven IIMs Reeling under Faculty Crunch." *ExpressBuzz*, December 10, 2008. http://www.expressbuzz.com/.

Singh, Nirvikir. "India's Information Technology Sector: What Contribution to Broader Economic Development?" OECD Development Centre. Working Paper no. 207, DEV/DOC(2003)05, March 2003.

Sikdar, Tapan. "Telecom Reforms in India." Presentation at the OECD Global Conference for Digital Policy for the Digital Economy, Dubai, January 2002.

Sood, Varun, and James Lamont. "India Looks to Restrict Senior Telecoms Jobs." *Financial Times*, August 11, 2009. http://www.ft.com/cms/ s/0/e26cab48-8697-11de-9e8e-00144feabdc0.html (subscription required).

Srivastava, Sadhana. "The Role of Foreign Direct Investment in India's Services Exports: An Empirical Investigation." *The Singapore Economic Review* 51, no. 2 (2006): 175–94.

State Bank of India. "Annual Results FY 09," May 13, 2009. http://www.statebankofindia.com/webfiles/uploads/files/Chairman-PPT-to-Analysts 130509.pdf.

Sunder, Shyam. "Yash Pal Committee Report on Higher Education: A Review." June 26, 2009. http://www.som.yale.edu /faculty/ sunder/

Research/India/Presentations%20and%20Working%20P   apers/Review-Yash-Pal-Report-Higher%20Education26Jun2009.pdf.

Telecom Regulatory Authority of India (TRAI). *The India Telecom Services Performance Indicators: October–December 2009*. New Delhi: TRAI, April 6, 2010. http://www.trai.gov.in/WriteReadData/trai/upload /Reports/50/IndicatorReport6apr10.pdf.

TeleGeography. *India*. Washington, DC: TeleGeography, April 30, 2010.

———. "Indian 3G Auction Closes: Seven of Nine Bidders Grab Concessions." *CommsUpdate*, May 25, 2010._http://www.telegeography. com/cu/article.php?article id=33174& email= html.

———. "India to Allow MVNOs." *CommsUpdate*, March 2, 2009.

———. *TeleGeography Report*. Washington, DC: TeleGeography, March 2009. ———. "Telstra Set to Revisit India Market." *CommsUpdate*, November 27, 2009.

Timmons, Heather, and Vikas Bajaj. "In Indian Airline's Troubles, a Cautionary Tale." *The New York Times*, June 19, 2009. http://www.newyorktimes.com/ (accessed June 18, 2009).

Tinbergen, Jan. *Shaping the World Economy*. New York: Twentieth Century Fund, 1962.

United Nations Educational, Scientific and Cultural Organization (UNESCO). *Global Education Digest 2006: Comparing Education Statistics Across the World*. Montreal, Canada: Institute for Statistics, 2006. http://www.uis.unesco.org/publications/ GED2006.

———. Institute for Statistics. *Global Education Digest 2009: Comparing Education Statistics Across the World*. Montreal, Canada: Institute for Statistics, 2009. http://www.uis.unesco.org/publications/GED2009.

University Grants Commission (UGC). "Territorial Jurisdiction of the State Universities/State Private Universities—Regarding." Notice to vice chancellors of all private universities, April 28, 2009, and to all state governments, April 16, 2009. http://www.ugc.ac.in/notices/teritorial.html.

U.S. Department of Commerce (USDOC). Bureau of Economic Analysis (BEA). Balance of Payments and Direct Investment Position database. http://www.bea.gov/international/ii   web/timeseries2.cfm?econtypeid= 2&dirlevel1id=1&Entityty peid=1&stepnum=1 (accessed July 28, 2010).

———. "Quarterly Survey of Transactions in Selected Services and Intangible Assets with Foreign Persons." Form BE-125.Washington, DC: BEA, January 2010. http://www.bea.gov/surveys/pdf/be125.pdf.

———. *Survey of Current Business* 84, no. 10 (October 2004).

————. *Survey of Current Business* 88, no. 10 (October 2008). http://www.bea.gov/scb/pdf/2008/10%20October/services text.pdf.

————. *Survey of Current Business* 89, no. 10 (October 2009).

————. *U.S. International Services: Cross-Border Trade 1986–2008, and Services Supplied Through Affiliates, 1986–2007.* "Table 2: Private Services Trade by Area and Country, 1992–2008." http://www.bea.gov/international/xls/tab2a.xls (accessed May 12, 2010).

————. *U.S. International Services: Cross-Border Trade, 1986–2008, and Services Supplied Through Affiliates, 1986–2007.* "Table 3: Travel, Passenger Fares, and Other Transportation, 1986–2008." http://www.bea.gov/international/xls/tab3.xls (accessed October 27, 2009).

————. *U.S. International Services: Cross-Border Trade 1986–2008, and Services Supplied Through Affiliates, 1986–2007.* "Table 5: Other Private Services" (1992-2005 dataset). http://www.bea.gov/international /xls/tab5b.xls (accessed October 1, 2009).

————. *U.S. International Services: Cross-Border Trade 1986–2008, and Services Supplied Through Affiliates, 1986–2007.* "Table 7: Business, Professional, and Technical Services." 2006–2008 dataset. http://www.bea.gov/international/xls/tab7a.xls (accessed October 1, 2009).

U.S. Department of Commerce (USDOC). International Trade Administration (ITA). "Healthcare Indicators" 2005. http://www.trade /td/healt/india_ indicators05.pdf (accessed August 31, 2009).

U.S. Department of Energy (USDOE). Energy Information Administration (EIA). "India: Electricity." *Country Analysis Briefs*, March 2009. http://www.eia.doe.gov/emeu/cabs/India/Electricity.html.

————. "India: Natural Gas." *Country Analysis Briefs*, March 2009. http://www.eia.doe.gov/emeu/cabs/India/NaturalGas.html.

————. International Energy Statistics database. http://tonto.eia.doe.gov /cfapps/ipdbproject/IEDIndex3.cfm (accessed May 17, 2010).

U.S. Department of Transportation (USDOT). Federal Aviation Administration (FAA). *FAA Aerospace Forecasts Fiscal Years 2009– 2025.* Washington, DC: FAA, 2009. http://www.faa.gov/data_research /aviation/aerospace_forecasts/2009- 2025/media/2009%20Forecast%20Doc.pdf.

U.S. International Trade Commission (USITC). "Computer and Related Services." *Recent Trends in U.S. Services Trade: 2007 Annual Report.* USITC Publication 3925. Washington, DC: USITC, June 2007.

Vishnoi, Anubhuti. "Back in India, Academics Apply to UGC for Teaching Jobs." *Indian Express*, May 28, 2009. http://www.indianexpress.com /news/back-in-india-academics-apply-to-ugc-forteaching-jobs/467152/.

Walsh, Keith. "Trade in Services: Does Gravity Hold? A Gravity Model Approach to Estimating Barriers to Services Trade." Institute for International Integration Studies. IIS Discussion Paper no. 183, October 2006.

Walters, Robert, Tim Stapleton, and Richard Andrews. *India's Services Sector: Unlocking Opportunity*. Canberra, Australia: Australian Government, Department of Foreign Affairs and Trade, Economic Analytical Unit, 2007.

Wood, Nick. "Indian Government Agrees to Sell 10% of BSNL." *Financial Times*, January 7, 2010. http://www.totaltele.com/view.aspx?ID= 451925&mail=168 (subscription required).

World Bank. "Country and Lending Groups." http://data.worldbank.org /about/countryclassifications/country-and-lending-groups#Low_income (accessed June 3, 2010).

———. Doing Business database. http://www.doingbusiness.org/ (accessed October 1, 2009).

———. *India Inclusive Growth and Service Delivery: Building on India's Success; Development Policy Review*. Report No. 34580-IN, May 29, 2006.

———. "India: Country Summary of Higher Education," n.d. http://siteresources.worldbank.org/EDUCATION/Resources/278200- 1121703274255/1439264- 1193249163062/India CountrySummary.pdf (accessed October 1, 2009).

———. World Development Indicators (WDI) Online database. http://ddp-ext.worldbank.org/ext/DDPQQ/member.do?method=getMembe rs&userid=1&queryId=6 (accessed various dates) (subscription required).

World Tourism Organization. *Collection of Tourism Expenditure Statistics*. Madrid: World Tourism Organization, 1995. http://pub.world-tourism.org /WebRoot/Store/Shops/Infoshop/Products/1034/1034-1.pdf.

World Trade Organization (WTO). "Communication from India: Draft Consolidated Schedule of Specific Commitments." S/DCS/W/IND, April 2, 2003.

———. General Agreement on Trade in Services (GATS). "India: Schedule of Specific Commitments." GATS/SC/42, April 15, 1994.

———. Services Statistics Database: India (accessed May 20, 2010).

WTO. Council for Trade in Services, Special Session. "India: Revised Offer." TN/S/O/IND/Rev.1, August 24, 2005. http://commerce.nic.in/trade/ international trade tis gaitis iootin.asp.

WTO Secretariat. *Trade Policy Review: Report by the Secretariat; India.* WT/TPR/S/182, April 18, 2007. http://www.wto.org/english/tratop_ e/tpr_e/tp283_e.htm.

————. *Trade Policy Review: Report by the Secretariat; India; Revision.* WT/TPR/S/182/Rev.1, July 24, 2007. http://docsonline.wto.org.

End Notes

[1] U.S. Department of Commerce (USDOC), Bureau of Economic Analysis (BEA), *U.S. International Services*, table 2 (accessed May 12, 2010). Data are not available for all trading partners.

[2] Ghani and Kharas, "The Service Revolution," May 2010, 2.

[3] The next paper will focus on Malaysia.

[4] This paper defines outsourcing as "the purchase of goods and services that were reviously produced inside the purchasing company" (Molnar, Pain, and Taglioni, "Globalisation and Employment in the OECD," 2008, 4). Firms in India's outsourcing industries serve both Indian and foreign companies. See box 1 for more on the definition of the IT–BPO industry.

[5] World Bank, World Development Indicators (WDI) Online database (accessed August 10, 2009); World Bank, "Country and Lending Groups," (accessed June 3, 2010). The World Bank classifies member countries by income level using gross national income (GNI) per capita. Countries classified as low income have annual GNI per capita of $975 or less; lower-middleincome countries, $975 to $3,856; upper-middle-income countries, $3,856 to $11,905; and high-income countries, $11,906 or greater. In July 2008, the World Bank changed its classification of India from a "low-income" to "lower-middle-income" country. The latest available data on services as a percentage of GDP growth in Thailand are for 2007.

[6] World Bank, WDI Online database (accessed August 10, 2009). The latest available data on value-added growth in Thailand's services sector are for 2007.

[7] Fernandez and Gupta, "Understanding the Growth Momentum in India's Services," 2006, 167.

[8] Fernandez and Gupta, "Understanding the Growth Momentum in India's Services," 2006, 170– 172. Indian national accounts data define business services to include software consultancy, data processing, and other computer-related services. See Government of India, Ministry of Statistics and Programme Implementation, Central Statistical Organization (CSO), *National Accounts Statistics: Sources and Methods*, March 2007, 168–170.

[9] CSO, *National Accounts Statistics, 2006–07,* May 2009, 75. The category of "community, social, and personal services" refers broadly to education, healthcare, social work, and hairdressing services, among other activities. "Transport, storage and communication" services include transportation services by air, land, or sea, postal and courier services, and telecommunication services. "Business and real estate services" refer to property leasing, the rental of machinery and transport equipment, advertising, architecture and engineering services, software consultancy, data processing, and other computer-related activities. For a

complete list of activities included within each service category, see CSO, *National Accounts Statistics: Sources and Methods,* March 2007, 168–170.

[10] World Bank, WDI Online database (accessed August 10, 2009). In this data source, the industrial sector includes mining and quarrying (including oil production), manufacturing, construction, and public utilities (electricity, gas, and water).

[11] Gordon and Gupta, "Understanding India's Services Revolution," September 2004, 8.

[12] World Bank, WDI Online database (accessed August 10, 2009). Data are for 2005.

[13] Singh, "India's Information Technology Sector," March 2003, 9. IT refers to the processing, storage, and transmission of information in digital form.

[14] Banga, "Critical Issues in India's Service-Led Growth," March 2005, 19; Gordon and Gupta, "Understanding India's Services Revolution," September 2004, 8. These studies note that improvements in technology and efficiency gains from liberalization probably have contributed to high productivity in the aforementioned industries.

[15] McKinsey & Company, *India: The Growth Imperative,* September 2001.

[16] World Bank, WDI Online database (accessed August 27, 2009). For example, during the period 1990–2001, GDP per capita in India, as measured in constant dollar terms for year 2000, increased by 48 percent; for the period 2002–07, by 43 percent. By contrast, U.S. GDP per capita during the period 1990–2001 increased by 22 percent; and for the period 2002–07, by 10 percent.

[17] USDOC, ITA, "Healthcare Indicators," 2005, 2.

[18] Hot Telecom, *Country Profile: India,* July 2009, 10.

[19] Pereira, "India: Not Just Another BRIC in the Wall," January 29, 2009, 20.

[20] Walters, Stapleton, and Andrews, *India's Services Sector: Unlocking Opportunity,* 2007, 18; and Gordon and Gupta, "Understanding India's Services Revolution," September 2004, 11.

[21] Leung, "Out of India: More American Companies Are Sending Jobs Overseas," August 1, 2004.

[22] Walters, Stapleton, and Andrews, *India's Services Sector: Unlocking Opportunity,* 2007, 18.

[23] *Economist,* "Bittersweet Synergy," October 22, 2009.

[24] Walters, Stapleton, and Andrews, *India's Services Sector: Unlocking Opportunity,* 2007, 9–10.

[25] Sikdar, "Telecom Reforms in India," January 2002.

[26] Walters, Stapleton, and Andrews, *India's Services Sector: Unlocking Opportunity,* 2007, 23.

[27] IndiaStat, "Growth of IT-ITES Professionals in India (1999–2000 to 2005–2006)," and "Employed Workers in Selected Industrys *[sic]* in India" (both accessed August 3, 2009). According to India's Ministry of Communications and Information Technology, data on employment in the IT sector include such activities as software engineering and R&D, the export of software products, and IT-enabled services. The data do not include employment related to computer hardware.

[28] IndiaStat, "Growth of IT-ITES Professionals in India (1999–2000 to 2005–2006)," and "Employed Workers in Selected Industrys *[sic]* in India" (accessed August 3, 2009).

[29] Walters, Stapleton, and Andrews, *India's Services Sector: Unlocking Opportunity,* 2007, 22–23. Average daily wages in India vary widely by industry, and are generally higher in services than in non-service sectors. For example, for the period 1993–2002, the average daily wage of a worker engaged in the manufacture of cotton textiles was 78 rupees; in the manufacture of aircraft and aircraft parts, 192 rupees; and in petroleum refining, 257 rupees. By contrast, in 2002, the average daily wage of a worker engaged in the provision of electricity services was 309 rupees, and in port services, 389 rupees. (Government of India, Labour Bureau, "Statistics: Occupational Wage Surveys," n.d.)

[30] Walters, Stapleton, and Andrews, *India's Services Sector: Unlocking Opportunity*, 2007, 22–23.

[31] Economist Intelligence Unit (EIU), *Country Profile: India*, 2008, 23.

[32] Walters, Stapleton, and Andrews, *India's Services Sector: Unlocking Opportunity*, 2007, 22–23.

[33] Reserve Bank of India (RBI), Database (accessed October 29, 2009).

[34] Government of India, Planning Commission, *Eleventh Five-Year Plan 2007–2012*, Vol. 1, 2008, 273.

[35] Poddar and Yi, "India's Rising Growth Potential," January 22, 2007, 3.

[36] Poddar and Yi, "India's Rising Growth Potential," January 22, 2007, 3.

[37] Srivastava, "The Role of Foreign Direct Investment in India's Services Exports," 2006, 175.

[38] Walters, Stapleton, and Andrews, *India's Services Sector: Unlocking Opportunity*, 2007, 7.

[39] Government of India, Planning Commission, *Eleventh Five-Year Plan 2007-2012*, Vol. 1, 2008, 273. Estimates of the sector's exports differ from source to source due to the use of different definitions for the sector (see box 1 on page 30).

[40] Kapur and Ramamurti, "India's Emerging Competitive Advantage in Services," 2001, 27.

[41] Poddar and Yi, "India's Rising Growth Potential," January 22, 2007, 16.

[42] Payscale, Salary Snapshot database.

[43] Walters, Stapleton, and Andrews, *India's Services Sector: Unlocking Opportunity*, 2007, 23.

[44] Software firms are not subject to industrial licensing by the Indian government. Kapur and Ramamurti, "India's Emerging Competitive Advantage in Services," 2001, 24.

[45] Kapur and Ramamurti, "India's Emerging Competitive Advantage in Services," 2001, 24.

[46] OECD, "Economic Survey of India, 2007," October 2007, 5.

[47] Mattoo, Mishra, and Shingal, "Sustaining India's Services Revolution," 2004, 30–31.

[48] Mattoo, Mishra, and Shingal, "Sustaining India's Services Revolution," 2004, 29.

[49] In 2007, only 41 percent of banks' assets could be allocated with complete freedom. OECD, "Economic Survey of India, 2007," October 2007, 7.

[50] World Bank, Doing Business database.

[51] Government of India, Planning Commission, *Eleventh Five-Year Plan 2007–2012*, Vol. 1, 2008, 274.

[52] Nayyar, "The Internationalization of Firms from India," March 2008, 126.

[53] A. T. Kearney, *The Shifting Geography of Offshoring*, 2009, 9. The Indian outsourcing company Satyam Computer Services was discovered in 2009 to have systematically falsified records of its earnings and assets for years.

[54] Ahluwalia, "Economic Reforms in India Since 1991," 2002, 72.

[55] *Economist*, "Ruled by Lakshmi," December 13, 2008.

[56] RBI, Database (accessed October 29, 2009).

[57] RBI, Database (accessed October 29, 2009).

[58] OECD, OECD.Stat Extracts: Trade in Services by Partner Country database (accessed October 1, 2009).

[59] USDOC, BEA, *U.S. International Services*, table 5 (accessed October 1, 2009).

[60] Baker, "Senate Approves Indian Nuclear Deal," October 1, 2008.

[61] Office of the United States Trade Representative (USTR), "United States and India Sign Framework for Cooperation on Trade and Investment," March 17, 2010.

[62] OECD, OECD.Stat Extracts: Trade in Services by Partner Country database (accessed October 1, 2009).

[63] In comparison, the United States and China have fewer institutional commonalities.

[64] Monger and Barr, "Nonimmigrant Admissions to the United States," April 2009, 5. Canadian and UK workers were a distant 2nd and 3rd.

[65] Herbst, "Indian Firms, Microsoft Top H-1B List," February 24, 2009.

[66] Kapur and Ramamurti, "India's Emerging Competitive Advantage in Services," 2001, 26.

[67] Lamont, "India Lashes Out at US Visa Regime," *Financial Times,* August 10, 2010.

[68] Kapur and Ramamurti, "India's Emerging Competitive Advantage in Services," 2001, 24.

[69] A. T. Kearney, *The Shifting Geography of Offshoring,* 2009, 3.

[70] Kapur and Ramamurti, "India's Emerging Competitive Advantage in Services," 2001, 26.

[71] Nayyar, "The Internationalization of Firms from India," March 2008, 121.

[72] Kapur and Ramamurti, "India's Emerging Competitive Advantage in Services," 2001, 23.

[73] Doig et al., "Has Outsourcing Gone Too Far?" 2001, 25.

[74] A. T. Kearney, *The Shifting Geography of Offshoring,* 2009, 9.

[75] Mattoo, Mishra, and Shingal, "Sustaining India's Services Revolution," 2004, 42.

[76] Srivastava, "The Role of Foreign Direct Investment in India's Services Exports," 2006, 191.

[77] WTO, GATS, "India: Schedule of Specific Commitments," April 15, 1994.

[78] WTO Secretariat, *Trade Policy Review: Report by the Secretariat; India; Revision,* July 24, 2007, 126.

[79] Government of India, Planning Commission, *Eleventh Five-Year Plan 2007-2012, Volume I,* 2008, 276.

[80] Mattoo and Subramanian, "India and the Multilateral Trading System Post-Doha," 2003, 327.

[81] USTR, "India," 2009, 242.

[82] Mode 1 refers to services delivered from the territory of the producer to the territory of the consumer.

[83] Mode 4 refers to services delivered by a supplier, present as a natural person, within the territory of the consumer.

[84] India's former chief trade negotiator Rahul Khullar has referred to mode 4 as India's most important market access area. Kanth, "Revised Text Needed for Doha Round Success," May 8, 2008.

[85] Specifically, India has requested that the United States "Remove the limitation [on entry of professionals] on account of narrow definition of specialty occupation which insists on 'higher specialised knowledge' or 'higher degree' of qualification both of which are not clearly specified" (Government of India, Ministry of Trade and Industry, Department of Commerce, "Trade in Services: Requests to Developed Countries; USA," n.d.). Meeting these demands would require extensive changes to the US immigration system, which would exceed the authority of the USTR.

[86] Mode 2 refers to services delivered in the territory of the supplier to a consumer from another territory.

[87] Mattoo, Mishra, and Shingal, "Sustaining India's Services Revolution," 2004, 23.

[88] Government of India, Ministry of Trade and Industry, Department of Commerce, "Trade Agreements," n.d.

[89] De Mel, "India–Sri Lanka," October 15, 2008.

[90] Bhuyan, "Saarc Meet to Fast-track Services Trade, Expand Safta Regulation," October 29, 2009.

[91] Sen, "India Seeks Demand List from Asean Nations," December 14, 2009.

[92] The APTA (formerly known as the Bangkok Agreement) is a preferential trading arrangement that includes Bangladesh, China, India, South Korea, Laos, and Sri Lanka.

[93] The 1988 Agreement on the Global System of Trade Preferences among Developing Countries promotes trade and economic cooperation among the Group of 77 developing countries.

[94] Government of India, Ministry of Trade and Industry, Department of Commerce, "Trade Agreements," n.d.

[95] Intraregional trade in South Asia was less than 2 percent of the combined GDP of countries in that region in 2007, compared to 20 percent in East Asia. Ahmed and Ghani, "South Asia's Growth and Regional Integration," 2007, 4.

[96] Government of India, Planning Commission, *Eleventh Five-Year Plan 2007-2012, Volume I,* 2008, 277.

[97] Government of India, Ministry of Trade and Industry, Department of Commerce, "Trade Agreements," n.d.

[98] Srivastava, "The Role of Foreign Direct Investment in India's Services Exports," 2006, 178.

[99] Walters, Stapleton, and Andrews, *India's Services Sector: Unlocking Opportunity,* 2007, 19.

[100] Ahluwalia, "Economic Reforms in India Since 1991," 2002, 72.

[101] Ahluwalia, "Economic Reforms in India Since 1991," 2002, 83.

[102] RBI, *RBI Bulletin,* July 2009, 1152.

[103] RBI, *RBI Bulletin,* July 2009, 1152.

[104] Mattoo, Mishra, and Shingal, "Sustaining India's Services Revolution," 2004, 26–29.

[105] *Economist,* "Storm-clouds Gathering," December 11, 2008.

[106] Mattoo, Mishra, and Shingal, "Sustaining India's Services Revolution," 2004, 35; *Economist,* "Not Entirely Free, Your Honour," July 31, 2010, 47.

[107] Helpman, Melitz, and Rubinstein, "Estimating Trade Flows," February 2007, 1.

[108] Tinbergen, "Shaping the World Economy," 1962.

[109] Grünfeld and Moxnes, "The Intangible Globalization," 2003.

[110] Kimura and Lee, "The Gravity Equation in International Trade in Services," April 2006.

[111] Grünfeld and Moxnes, "The Intangible Globalization," 2003, 7.

[112] Some models use only the share of GDP accounted for by the sector being studied. We ran an alternative model using the service sector's share of GDP instead of overall GDP, and found similar results, but with a smaller effect of FDI barriers on imports of services. We use overall GDP to reflect the fact that traded services are often intermediate inputs in the production of goods as well as services.

[113] Kimura and Lee, "The Gravity Equation in International Trade in Services," 2006, 95.

[114] Walsh, "Trade in Services," October 2006.

[115] Grünfeld and Moxnes use Trade Restrictiveness Indexes (TRIs) for six service industries developed by the Australian Productivity Commission (APC). Kimura and Lee use the Economic Freedom of the World Index developed by the Fraser Institute. Walsh uses the Heritage Foundation's Index of Economic Freedom, measures of government effectiveness developed by Kaufmann et al. of the World Bank, the APC TRIs, and measures based on GATS commitments developed by Hoekman (1995). Walsh runs sector-specific regressions as well as ones for all services trade.

[116] Golub, "Openness to Foreign Direct Investment in Services," 2009.

[117] The literature examining the relationship between FDI and cross-border trade in goods is more extensive than for services. Some of these studies point to substitutive effects as well. See, for example, Blonigen, "In Search of Substitution between Foreign Production and Exports," February 2001, and Helpman et al., "Export versus FDI," January 2003.

[118] Fillat-Castejón, Francois, and Wörz, "Cross-Border Trade and FDI in Services," February 2009, 10, 17, 20–21.

[119] Grünfeld and Moxnes, "The Intangible Globalization," 2003, 20–21.

[120] The remoteness variable has been calculated similarly in a number of previous studies. Often, the distance between *i* and bilateral trading partner *j* is excluded in the summation of all

trading partners, m. Doing so would introduce only a slight change in the values of our remoteness variable due to the number of observations in our model. Anderson and Van Wincoop argue that remoteness has little explanatory power and should be replaced by a broader measure ("multilateral resistance") that accounts for the full range of differences in relative trade costs (Anderson and Van Wincoop, "Gravity with Gravitas," March 2003, 5–6). Baier and Bergstrand simplify this measurement using a Taylor-series expansion (Baier and Bergstrand, "*Bonus Vetus* OLS," 2009, 78–80). Both models require the strong assumption that trade costs are symmetric; that is, the cost of exporting from country i to j is approximately equivalent to the cost of exporting from country j to i. Even if the assumption does not hold for every pair of trading partners, the use of data that include bilateral trade flows can balance out the effects of any asymmetries. However, in our dataset, non-OECD countries appear solely as importers, so we do not have bilateral flows for many country pairs. Therefore, we proceed using the more traditional specification of remoteness.

[121] A random effects model allows one to estimate coefficients for variables that do not vary over time, such as SFDIR. Fixed effects and first differences, two other common methods for analyzing panel data, do not permit analysis of time-invariant variables. The random effects model requires the assumption that the effects of any unobserved variables are uncorrelated with the independent variables in the model.

[122] The year dummies control for factors specific to those years that may have affected trade among all countries.

[123] OECD, OECD.Stat Extracts: Trade in Services by Partner Country database (accessed August 2009).

[124] OECD, OECD.Stat Extracts: Trade in Services by Partner Country database (accessed August 2009).

[125] RBI, *Reserve Bank of India Annual Report,* August 27, 2009, 172.

[126] Chadwick, "Global Trends in Information Technology Outsourcing," November 2003, 4.

[127] NASSCOM, *Strategic Review 2009*, February 2009, 203.

[128] The Indian fiscal year ends on March 31st. Fiscal year 2011 began on April 1, 2010.

[129] NASSCOM, *Strategic Review 2009*, February 2009, 44. These figures include revenues from exports (IT services, software, products engineering, research and development, BPO, and hardware) and the domestic market (hardware, IT services, software products, and BPO). In FY 2008, revenue from hardware sales accounted for 1.2 percent of the industry's total exports and 49.6 percent of domestic revenue (NASSCOM, *Strategic Review 2009*, February 2009, 203).

[130] NASSCOM, *Strategic Review 2009*, February 2009, 216. Approximately 860,000 people were employed in the IT services export sector; 700,000 in the BPO export sector; and 450,000 in the domestic IT-BPO sector. The estimates do not include employees in the IT hardware sector.

[131] NASSCOM, *Strategic Review 2009*, February 2009, 53.

[132] Dataquest, *DQ Top20,* July 11, 2009; Dataquest, *The DQ BPO Top20*, July 25, 2009.

[133] NASSCOM, *Strategic Review 2009*, February 2009, 50. The figure quoted here includes software. NASSCOM's export statistics include revenues from foreign subsidiaries of Indian companies. Its figures typically differ from those prepared by the Reserve Bank of India, which do not include such revenues (NASSCOM, *Strategic Review 2009: The IT-BPO Sector in India*, 2009, 44).

[134] Dun & Bradstreet, "India's Top IT Companies," 2008.

[135] NASSCOM describes Continental Europe as including "nations such as Germany, France, the Benelux region, and the Nordic countries." NASSCOM, *Strategic Review 2009*, February 2009, 56.

[136] Total IT-BPO exports to Continental Europe reached $5.3 billion in FY 2008. NASSCOM, *Strategic Review 2009*, February 2009, 56.

[137] NASSCOM, *Strategic Review 2010*, February 2010, 6, 55–56.

[138] WTO Secretariat, *Trade Policy Review*, April 18, 2007, 125.

[139] WTO, Council for Trade in Services, Special Session, "India: Revised Offer," August 24, 2005. The proposed commitment applies to all "computer and related services" (category 84 of the United Nations Provisional Central Product Classification). India's existing GATS schedule includes a binding commitment to allow foreign equity of up to 51 percent in the following activities: consultancy services related to the installation of computer hardware, software implementation services, data processing services, database services, and maintenance and repair services of office machinery and equipment including computers (WTO, "Communication from India," April 2, 2003, 5).

[140] RBI, *Annual Report,* August 27, 2009, 180. The total is for the industry defined by RBI as "computer services." The report does not list the shares of FDI by country, but the U.S. share may have been substantial. U.S. direct investment capital outflows to India in "professional, scientific, and technical services," a category which includes many computer-enabled services, totaled $356 million in calendar year 2007. USDOC, BEA, Balance of Payments and Direct Investment Position database.

[141] Gartner, "Gartner Says," June 9, 2009. In 2008, by revenue, the top three global IT service providers were based in the United States: IBM ($58.9 billion), Hewlett Packard ($38.6 billion), and Accenture ($23.7 billion).

[142] Cloud computing refers to the delivery of computer applications over the Internet. The "cloud" is the network of data centers where these applications are housed. *Economist*, "Clash of the Clouds," October 15, 2009.

[143] IBM, "IBM Opens Four Cloud Computing Centers," September 24, 2008.

[144] Cathers, *Industry Surveys*, May 2009, 10.

[145] NASSCOM, *Strategic Review 2009*, February 2009, 76.

[146] NASSCOM, *Strategic Review 2009*, February 2009, 206–14.

[147] NASSCOM, *Strategic Review 2009*, February 2009, 50, 110–11.

[148] Dun & Bradstreet, "India's Top IT Companies 2008,"February 2008.

[149] NASSCOM, *Strategic Review 2009*, February 2009, 174.

[150] NASSCOM, *Strategic Review 2010*, February 2010, 6.

[151] Heath, "Mahindra Satyam Boss Talks Up Prospects," *Bloomberg Businessweek,* August 11, 2009.

[152] Cathers, *Industry Surveys*, October 2009, 4–5.

[153] A.T. Kearney, *The Shifting Geography of Offshoring*, 2009, 1–9.

[154] NASSCOM, *Strategic Review 2009*, February 2009, 78–80.

[155] *Economist*, "Bittersweet Synergy," October 22, 2009.

[156] NASSCOM, *Strategic Review 2009*, February 2009, 82.

[157] Roy et al., "Wipro Infotech Wins IT Outsourcing Deal with Aircel," April 1, 2008.

[158] Dun & Bradstreet, "India's Top IT Companies 2008," February 2008.

[159] Holman, Batt, and Holtgrewe, "The Global Call Center Report," 2007, 37.

[160] McKinsey and Company and NASSCOM, *NASSCOM-McKinsey Report*, 2005, 16; Cathers, *Industry Surveys*, October 2009, 12. In 2008, the average yearly salary for an IT worker in India was $14,270, which was above the average in Vietnam ($13,240), but below the

average in the Philippines ($14,710) and well below the averages in developed countries (e.g., the average salary for a U.S. IT worker was $81,520). These figures are from a survey of over 35,000 IT workers worldwide; the training, experience, and professional responsibilities of respondents varied. Gilmore et al., "Salary Survey 2008," December 2008.

[161] Cathers, *Industry Surveys*, October 2009, 12.

[162] NASSCOM, *Strategic Review 2010*, February 2010, 9.

[163] McKinsey and Company and NASSCOM, *Perspective 2020*, April 2009, 21.

[164] McKinsey and Company and NASSCOM, *NASSCOM-McKinsey Report*, 2005, 16.

[165] McKinsey and Company and NASSCOM, *Perspective 2020*, April 2009, 27.

[166] NASSCOM, *Strategic Review 2009*, February 2009, 125.

[167] Gera, "IT Players Concerned Over Extension of STPI Act," March 12, 2009.

[168] Walters, Stapleton, and Andrews, *India's Services Sector: Unlocking Opportunity*, 2007, 53; Hot Telecom, *Country Profile: India*, July 2009, 13.

[169] Throughout this chapter, penetration is defined as the number of telephone lines and/or subscribers per 100 inhabitants.

[170] TRAI, *The Indian Telecom Services Performance Indicators,* April 6, 2010, i, 4.

[171] Ministry of Communications and Information Technology (MoC) Web site, http://www.mit.gov.in (accessed October 26, 2009). The Department of Information Technology is responsible for policy pertaining to Internet services.

[172] Belgaonkar and Chinta, *India,* April 15, 2009, 6. The Telecom Commission was created by the MoC in 1989. Together, the Telecom Commission and the DoT are responsible for policy formulation, licensing, and wireless spectrum management.

[173] Belgaonkar and Chinta, *India*, April 15, 2009, 6–7.

[174] WTO Secretariat, *Trade Policy Review: India*, April 18, 2007, 134; Wood, "Indian Government Agrees to Sell 10% of BSNL," January 7, 2010. In January 2010, the Indian government agreed to sell a 10 percent stake in BSNL.

[175] Belgaonkar and Chinta, *India*, April 15, 2009, 7.

[176] WTO Secretariat, *Trade Policy Review: India*, April 18, 2007, 135. The TRAI regulates tariffs for services deemed uncompetitive, including rural fixed-line telephone calls, national mobile roaming, and leased circuits. Tariffs for all other telecommunication services are fully liberalized.

[177] TRAI Web site, http://www.trai.gov.in (accessed October 26, 2009).

[178] The Indian Telegraph Act, 1885, part II, paragraphs 4, 6A, and 7 and part III, paragraph 10, http://www.dot.gov.in/Acts/telegraphact.htm.

[179] Department of Telecommunications (DoT) Web site, http://www.dot.gov.in/Acts/act.htm (accessed May 10, 2010).

[180] DOT, "National Telecom Policy 1994," http://www.dot.gov.in/ntp/ntp1994.htm.

[181] DOT, "New Telecom Policy 1999," http://www.dot.gov.in/ntp/ntp1999.htm; TeleGeography, *India*, April 30, 2010.

[182] DoT Web site, http://www.dot.gov.in (accessed May 10, 2010); Belgaonkar and Chinta, *India*, April 15, 2009, 10 and 13; TeleGeography, *India*, April 30, 2010.

[183] Krishna, "India's TRAI Asks Govt Not to Issue New Licenses," August 5, 2009; TeleGeography, *India*, April 30, 2010.

[184] Belgaonkar and Chinta, *India*, April 15, 2009, 17.

[185] Business Monitor International Limited (BMI), *India Telecommunications Report,* September 2009, 47.

[186] WTO, "Communication from India," April 2, 2003, 11.

[187] WTO, Council for Trade in Services, Special Session, "India: Revised Offer," August 24, 2005.

[188] WTO Secretariat, *Trade Policy Review: India*, April 18, 2007, 134. In these sectors, foreign firms listed outside India are required to divest 26 percent of equity to the Indian public within five years. The term dark fiber refers to installed fiber optic cabling that is unused.

[189] WTO Secretariat, *Trade Policy Review: India*, April 18, 2007, 135. Foreign investment in bandwidth, paging, and ISP services is contingent upon DoT approval, subject to licensing and security requirements.

[190] Evans, *India*, June 2009, 23–25; TeleGeography, *India*, April 30, 2010; WTO Secretariat, *Trade Policy Review: India*, April 18, 2007, 135. Foreign equity positions larger than 49 percent require the approval the DoT and the Foreign Investment Promotion Board. To address security concerns, the Indian government imposes the following conditions on foreign equity positions exceeding 49 percent: (1) the chief executive officer, chairman of the board, and a majority of the company's shareholders must be Indian nationals; (2) domestic telephone traffic cannot be routed abroad; (3) customer and account information cannot be sent abroad; (4) servers, networks, and databases cannot be accessed from abroad for repair or maintenance.

[191] WTO Secretariat, *Trade Policy Review: India,* April 18, 2007, 134.

[192] TeleGeography, *India*, April 2010.

[193] TRAI, *The Indian Telecom Services Performance Indicators,* April 6, 2010, 15 and 18.

[194] TRAI, *The Indian Telecom Services Performance Indicators,* April 6, 2010, i.

[195] TRAI, *The Indian Telecom Services Performance Indicators,* April 6, 2010, 16.

[196] Hot Telecom, *Country Profile: India*, July 2009, 10.

[197] TRAI, *The Indian Telecom Services Performance Indicators,* April 6, 2010, 18.

[198] BMI, *India Telecommunications Report*, September 2009, 23–24; TeleGeography, *India*, April 30, 2010; and Hot Telecom, *Country Profile: India*, July 2009, 16. The decline in total fixed lines in India also resulted from the reclassification of services delivered via wireless in the local loop and fixed wireless access technologies from the fixed-line sector to the wireless sector.

[199] Hot Telecom, *Country Profile: India*, July 2009, 10.

[200] TRAI, *The Indian Telecom Services Performance Indicators,* April 6, 2010, ix and 22.

[201] Gupta, *Trends in 2010: India Telecoms Market*, February 3, 2010, 9; Hot Telecom, *Country Profile India*, July 2009, 13.

[202] Hot Telecom, *Country Profile: India*, July 2009, 10.

[203] Hot Telecom, *Country Profile: India*, July 2009, 33–34.

[204] TRAI, *The Indian Telecom Services Performance Indicators,* April 6, 2010, 24.

[205] Hot Telecom, *Country Profile: India*, July 2009, 10.

[206] TRAI, *The Indian Telecom Services Performance Indicators*, April 6, 2010, ix. Industry analysts estimate that the number of mobile phone users in India could be up to 40 percent lower than that reported in official statistics, largely because many Indian customers purchase multiple SIM cards, a large portion of which are "lifetime" cards that are considered to be active even when no longer used. Some mobile service operators are also reportedly sending SIM cards to retailers that are activated before being sold to end users. Leahy, "India's Mobile Sector Gets a Reality Check," March 2, 2010.

[207] Belgaonkar and Chinta, *India*, April 15, 2009, 6.

[208] Mobile penetration exceeding 100 percent indicates that some mobile service customers own more than one mobile phone or SIM card.

[209] TRAI, *The Indian Telecom Services Performance Indicators,* April 6, 2010, i.

[210] TeleGeography, *India*, March 31, 2009.

[211] TRAI, *The Indian Telecom Services Performance Indicators,* April 6, 2010, 9. The remaining mobile services companies—MTNL, Sistema Shyam, Loop Mobile, Unitech, HFCL, and S Tel—each accounted for less than 1 percent of India's mobile services market at the end of 2009.

[212] TeleGeography, *India*, April 30, 2010.

[213] Leahy, "A Tough Call," May 25, 2010, 9. The large costs associated with Vodafone's recent acquisition of frequency spectrum was also cited as a factor in the write-down of its investment in Vodafone.

[214] Leahy, "A Tough Call," May 25, 2010, 9.

[215] Krishna, Guha, and Gulati, "Indian Regulator Recommends Easing Merger Rules," May 2010.

[216] Leahy, "A Tough Call," May 25, 2010, 9; Krishna, Guha, and Gulati, "Indian Regulator Recommends Easing Merger Rules," May 2010. Some analysts believe that, if implemented, the TRAI's recommendations would effectively restrict M&A activity to small and medium-sized operators, most of which do not have sufficient cash reserves to undertake a large purchase.

[217] TeleGeography, "India to Allow MVNOs," March 2, 2009. Mobile virtual network operators offer mobile services by purchasing wholesale voice minutes, or otherwise leasing network capacity, from mobile services companies that own and operate physical network infrastructure. As of June 2010, the government of India was in the process of developing MVNO guidelines. *Reuters*, "India Working on MVNO Guidelines-Telecom Secy," June 25, 2010.

[218] Lennighan, "Friday Review: Into India," September 25, 2009. In July 2010, the DOT stated that mobile number portability would be implemented by October 31, 2010. Ribeiro, "India Delays Mobile Number Portability Again," July 1, 2010.

[219] Gupta, *Trends in 2010: India Telecoms Market*, February 3, 2010, 5–6.

[220] BMI, *India Telecommunications Report*, September 2009, 39.

[221] Guha, Krishna, and Machado, "India's Wireless Broadband Auction Ends," June 11, 2010. In June 2010, the Indian government also concluded an auction for two slots of bandwidth to provide broadband wireless Internet services. Of the eleven pre-approved bidders, seven companies—Infotel Broadband Services, Aircel, Tikona Digitel Networks, Qualcomm, Bharti Airtel, and Augere—successfully bid for licenses, with Infotel obtaining a license in all 22 circles. In total, the government of India will receive approximately $8.2 billion from the auction.

[222] TeleGeography, "Indian 3G Auction Closes: Seven of Nine Bidders Grab Concessions," May 20, 2010. Of the nine preapproved bidders, Etisalat and Videocon did not obtain 3G licenses.

[223] Krishna and Guha, "BSNL, MTNL Have Cash to Meet 3G Bandwidth Fees," May 20, 2010.

[224] Middleton, "India's 3G Licensing Auction Finally Over," May 20, 2010.

[225] Sanders, "The German and Indian Spectrum Auctions: Did Operators Get Value for Money?" May 24, 2010; Middleton, "India's 3G Licensing Auction Finally Over," May 20, 2010.

[226] Leahy, "A Tough Call," May 25, 2010; Krishna and Guha, "BSNL, MTNL Have Cash to Meet 3G Bandwidth Fees," May 20, 2010; Gupta, *Trends in 2010: Indian Telecoms Market*, February 3, 2010, 8–9.

[227] Saadi, "Batelco Begins Telecom Operations in India," December 16, 2009; TeleGeography, *TeleGeography Report*, March 2009; BMI, *India Telecommunications Report,* September 2009, 32–33; Heng, "Singtel Increases Stake In India's Bharti Airtel," November 2, 2009.

[228] TeleGeography, *India*, April 30, 2010.

[229] BMI, *India Telecommunications Report*, September 2009, 46.

[230] TeleGeography, "Telstra Set to Revisit Indian Market," November 27, 2009.

[231] Leahy, "Bharti Seals Deal for Zain Networks," March 30, 2010; Middleton, "India's Bharti Moves into Bangladesh," January 12, 2010.

[232] Krishna, "BSNL Looking to Buy Small Companies Abroad," December 3, 2009; Dow Jones Newswires, "MTNL Eyes African Market," January 20, 2010.

[233] Dharmakumar and Prasad, "Bharti Minutes in Africa," April 28, 2010; Gupta, *Trends in 2010: India Telecoms Market*, February 3, 2010, 13.

[234] TeleGeography, *TeleGeography Report*, March 2009.

[235] USDOC, BEA, *Survey of Current Business*, 52–53.

[236] USTR, "India," April 2010.

[237] Sood and Lamont, "India Looks to Restrict Senior Telecoms Jobs," August 11, 2009.

[238] U.S. Department of Energy (USDOE), Energy Information Administration (EIA), International Energy Statistics database (accessed May 17, 2010).

[239] Walters, Stapleton, and Andrews, *India's Services Sector: Unlocking Opportunity*, 2007, 103.

[240] USDOE, EIA, International Energy Statistics database. Distribution losses may be the result of technical or nontechnical losses. Technical losses occur in the form of heat lost over long distances between electricity production and consumption centers. When voltage lines are too thin, the result is greater pressure and higher electricity loss. Technical losses occur in every electricity transmission and distribution system, and may be minimized by incorporating advanced technology and equipment, technically proficient management, and scheduled maintenance. Nontechnical losses result from activities such as illegally taking electricity from distribution lines, theft of distribution equipment, tampering with electricity meters, or distributors' failure to replace old or faulty electricity meters.

[241] World Bank, WDI Online database (accessed May 17, 2010). Regional averages reflect World Bank country classifications for regions.

[242] Government of India, Planning Commission, *Integrated Energy Policy*, August 2006, 2–3.

[243] EIU, "India Energy: Piecemeal Reforms," June 1, 2009.

[244] Scully, *Global Industry Surveys,* April 2007, 8.

[245] OECD, *OECD Economic Surveys: India,* October 2007, 203–07.

[246] USDOE, EIA, "India: Electricity," March 2009.

[247] USDOE, EIA, International Energy Statistics database (accessed May 17, 2010).

[248] Ramanathan, "AES Lines Up Largest Investment in Power," June 18, 2007; AES Corporation Web site, http://www.aes.com/aes/index?page=country&cat=IN (accessed August 31, 2009); China Light and Power Web site, https://www.clpgroup.com (accessed August 31, 2009); Bureau van Dijk, Orbis database (accessed September 16, 2009).

[249] USDOE, EIA, International Energy Statistics database; USITC staff calculations.

[250] Bureau van Dijk, Orbis database (accessed August 2009).

[251] EIU, "India: Energy Report," May 26, 2009.

[252] OECD, *OECD Economic Surveys: India,* October 2007, 207.

[253] EIU, "India Coal," June 12, 2009; EIU, "India: Energy Report," May 26, 2009.

[254] Scully, *Global Industry Surveys,* April 2007, 8–9.

[255] Scully, *Global Industry Surveys,* April 2007, 9; OECD, *OECD Economic Surveys: India,* October 2007, 205–06.

[256] OECD, *OECD Economic Surveys: India,* October 2007, 207. Although private sector participation in transmission and distribution is technically allowed under the 2003 Electricity Act, significant private sector participation would likely arise through purchases

of existing state-owned transmission and distribution assets rather than attempts to create new, privately owned grids.

[257] Jog, "NTPC to Follow National Tariff Policy," August 20, 2009; World Bank, *India Inclusive Growth and Service Delivery*, May 29, 2006, 86; OECD, *OECD Economic Surveys: India,* October 2007, 205.

[258] Staff estimates based on information from Directorate General of Civil Aviation, Statistical Division, *India Air Transport Statistics, 2007–2008*, April 2009, 27; and U.S. Department of Transportation (USDOT), Federal Aviation Administration (FAA), *FAA Aerospace Forecasts, Fiscal Years 2009–2025*, 2009, 10. The proceeding discussion will focus on the air passenger rather than the air cargo market. Data presented within this section pertain to air passenger transport only. See box 3 for a summary of developments in the air freight industry.

[259] Directorate General of Civil Aviation, Statistical Division, *India Air Transport Statistics, 2007–2008*, April 2009, 27. Data is reported for the period ending March 31, 2008.

[260] Directorate General of Civil Aviation, Statistical Division, *India Air Transport Statistics, 2007–2008*, April 2009, 26–27; Directorate General of Civil Aviation,"Category-wise Personnel Statistics of Scheduled Indian Carriers," n.d. Data on operating revenue is reported for the period ending March 31, 2008; on total employees, it is reported for the period ending March 31, 2007.

[261] Staff estimates based on data from CSO, *Statistical Abstract of India 2007*, 283; Directorate General of Civil Aviation, Statistical Division, *India Air Transport Statistics, 2007–08*, 26–27.

[262] *Economist*, "Flight to Value," August 8, 2009, 58.

[263] *IBA Newswatch,* "India's Budget Airlines Leave Rivals in Vapour Stream," September 11, 2009, 8; staff estimates based on data from Directorate General for Civil Aviation, "Airline-wise Financial Status of All Scheduled Indian Carriers," n.d. Data on operating revenue is reported for the period ending March 31, 2007.

[264] Walters, Stapleton, and Andrews, *India's Services Sector: Unlocking Opportunity*, 2007, 35.

[265] Directorate General of Civil Aviation, Statistical Division, *India Air Transport Statistics, 2007–08*, April 2009, 26–27; Directorate General of Civil Aviation, "Airline-wise Financial Status of All Scheduled Indian Carriers," n.d. Air India was originally established as the government's international carrier, whereas Indian Air served as its primary domestic carrier. In 1999, Indian Air established a low-cost subsidiary, Alliance Air, to compete with private, low-cost airlines, while in 2005, Air India established Air India Express to compete more effectively with foreign airlines transporting passengers between India and foreign markets.

[266] Directorate General of Civil Aviation, "Domestic Passengers Carried by Air India and Private Airlines in India (2005 to 2008)," n.d.; Government of India, Ministry of Finance, "Civil Aviation," 2009, 242. The newly merged airline is referred to under the brand name "Air India." Data on market share is for the period ending October 2008.

[267] Directorate General of Civil Aviation, "Airline-wise Financial Status of All Scheduled Indian Carriers," n.d.; Jet Airways, "Fact Sheet," via Jet Airways company Web site. http://www.jetairways.com (accessed September 24, 2009); various press releases via Kingfisher company Web site, http://www.flykingfisher.com/media-center/press-releases.aspx/ (accessed September 28, 2009).

[268] O'Connell and Williams, "Transformation of India's Domestic Airlines," 2006, 363.

[269] Directorate General of Civil Aviation, Statistical Division, *India Air Transport Statistics, 2007–08*, April 2009, 27.

[270] Gohain, "Airline Operations Regulatory Issues in India," n.d. Government regulations on the operation of domestic air transport services in India require (1) that an airline have its principal place of business registered in India; (2) that its chairman and two-thirds of its board of directors be Indian citizens; and (3) that Indian nationals have substantial ownership and control of the airline.

[271] O'Connell and Williams, "Transformation of India's Domestic Airlines," 2006, 359–60; Directorate General of Civil Aviation, Statistical Division, *India Air Transport Statistics, 2007–08*, April 2009, 28. In fiscal year 2007–08, India's domestic carriers reportedly accounted for 33 percent of passenger traffic between India and foreign countries.

[272] O'Connell and Williams, "Transformation of India's Domestic Airlines," 2006, 361. Air Deccan, India's first low-cost carrier began operating in August 2003.

[273] *People's Daily Online,* "Indian Civil Aviation Giant Jet Airways Acquires Air Sahara," January 20, 2006; *The Hindu,* "Jet Acquires Air Sahara Finally," April 13, 2007.

[274] *Case Studies and Management Resources,* "Kingfisher Airlines Acquires a Stake in Air Deccan," August 22, 2007.

[275] Directorate General of Civil Aviation, Statistical Division, *India Air Transport Statistics, 2007–08*, April 2009, 27; O'Connell and Williams, "Transformation of India's Domestic Airlines," 2006, 360.

[276] O'Connell and Williams, "Transformation of India's Domestic Airlines," 2006, 363.

[277] OECD, *OECD Statistics on International Trade in Services*, 2008.

[278] USDOC, BEA, *U.S. International Services,* table 3 (accessed October 27, 2009). U.S. exports of passenger fares to India principally reflect the transport of Indian residents on U.S. airlines' flights to and from the United States and India, whereas U.S. imports of passenger fares from India reflect the transport of U.S. citizens on Indian airlines.

[279] USDOC, BEA, *U.S. International Services,* table 3 (accessed October 27, 2009). In 2008, U.S. travel payments to India were nearly $2.4 billion, compared to $3.0 billion in U.S. travel receipts from India. In general, U.S. travel payments are calculated based on the purchase of goods and services by U.S. residents traveling abroad (excluding passenger fares), whereas U.S. travel receipts are based on the purchase of goods and services by foreign residents traveling in the United States.

[280] Directorate General of Civil Aviation, "Domestic Air Transport Policy," http://dgca.nic.in/ (accessed October 14, 2009).

[281] Hooper, "Liberalisation of the Airline Industry in India," 1997, 116–17.

[282] WTO, Council for Trade in Services, Special Session, "India: Revised Offer," August 24, 2005, 55.

[283] Timmons and Bajaj, "In Indian Airline's Troubles, a Cautionary Tale," June 19, 2009.

[284] Directorate General of Civil Aviation, "Procedure for Starting Scheduled/Non-Scheduled Air Transport Services," n.d. http://civilariation.nic.in/domesticairtransport.html (accessed October 5, 2009). The Indian Government repealed the Air Corporation Act (1953) on March 1, 1994. Among other things, the act had granted a monopoly on domestic air transport services to India's national airlines.

[285] Hooper, "Liberalisation of the Airline Industry in India," 1997, 116–17; Gohain, "Airline Operations Regulatory Issues in India," n.d. Government regulations that essentially required new-entrant carriers to operate a combination of lucrative and nonlucrative routes limited their success, however, and several airlines subsequently withdrew from the market.

[286] Hooper, "Liberalisation of the Airline Industry in India," 1997, 121.

[287] Directorate General of Civil Aviation, Statistical Division, *India Air Transport Statistics, 2007–08*, April 2009, 26.

[288] Gohain, "Airline Operations Regulatory Issues in India," n.d.

[289] Government of India, Ministry of Civil Aviation, *Annual Report, 2008–09*, September 2009, 6–7.

[290] Walters, Stapleton, and Andrews, *India's Services Sector: Unlocking Opportunity*, 2007, 34; Government of India, Ministry of Civil Aviation, *Annual Report, 2008–09*, September 2009, 8.

[291] Bisignani, Speech delivered to the Confederation of Indian Industry, September 24, 2008.

[292] Farrell and Beinhocker, "Next Big Spenders: India's Middle Class," May 19, 2007. India's middle class population is approximately 50 million, or roughly 4 percent of the total population. By 2025, the middle class population in India is estimated to grow to 583 million.

[293] Ionides, "India Unleashed," July 2006, 35–37.

[294] Directorate General of Civil Aviation, Statistical Division, *India Air Transport Statistics, 2007–08*, April 2009; World Bank, WDI database (accessed October 7, 2009).

[295] Air India, "Management Discussion and Analysis Report," 16.

[296] World Tourism Organization, "Collection of Tourism Expenditure Statistics," 1995, 4; RBI, *Reserve Bank of India Annual Report,* August 27, 2009, 115. Inbound to urists in India refer to foreign visitors to that country, whereas outbound tourists refer to Indian residents traveling abroad. During the period 2000–2004, Indian outbound tourism grew at an average annual rate of 7 percent, inbound tourism, 9 percent.

[297] Government of India, Ministry of Civil Aviation, *Annual Report, 2008–09*, September 2009, 5. Bilateral air services agreements permit airlines from two signatory countries to serve each other's markets, but place certain limitations on the routes that airlines may fly.

[298] IndiaStat, "Growth of Student Enrolment in Universities and Colleges of India" (accessed September 1, 2009); IndiaStat, "State-wise Number of Higher Educational Institutions in India, 2006–2007" (accessed September 1, 2009); Government of India, Ministry of Human Resource Development, *Annual Report 2007–08*, 2008, 118; Agarwal, "Higher Education in India," June 2006, 5.

[299] Government of India, Ministry of Human Resource Development, *Annual Report 2007–08*, 2008, 282. In 2005, the cumulative dropout rate was 26 percent through grade 5, 49 percent through grade 8, and 62 percent through grade 10. Nevertheless, these dropout rates have decreased substantially since 1970.

[300] Lakshman, "India to Foreign Colleges," July 31, 2009.

[301] Cheney, Ruzzi, and Muralidharan, "A Profile of the Indian Education System," November 2005, 20.

[302] Agarwal, "Higher Education in India," June 2006, 9; Government of India, Ministry of Human Resource Development, *Annual Report 2007–08*, 119–120. India's central government has declared certain higher education institutions in India deemedto-be universities, as provided for in section 3 of the University Grants Commission (UGC) Act of 1956. These institutions are authorized to award degrees by virtue of offering renowned, advanced programs in one or more particularly important or specialized fields of study. The number of deemed-to-be universities in India has substantially increased in recent years, as the government has widened the scope of designated institutions to include new and privately managed and financed institutions, a departure from the initial practice in the late 1950s of designating only public institutions.

[303] IGNOU, "IGNOU Profile 2008," 2008; Government of India, Ministry of Human Resource Development, *Annual Report 2007–08*, 206. Other universities (whether campus-based or online) in India are much smaller, enrolling approximately 500–600 students, on average.

[304] Programs of study lead to the award of competency certificates, diplomas, and bachelor's, master's, and doctoral degrees.

[305] Colleges in India award certificates or other acknowledgements of student achievement, but not degrees officially recognized in India, which are solely the responsibility of universities with which the colleges are affiliated.

[306] Government of India, Ministry of Human Resource Development, *Annual Report 2007–08*, 158.

[307] Levy, "Indian Private Higher Education in Comparative Perspective," October 2008, 5, 7. Private universities in India enroll less than 10 percent of total Indian university students.

[308] Agarwal, "Higher Education in India," June 2006, 13, 156.

[309] Levy, "Access through Private Higher Education," April 2008, 5; World Bank, "India: Country Summary of Higher Education," n.d., 15. Tuition and fees from a student's family are the principal source of funds at private higher education institutions in India.

[310] Kapur and Mehta, *"Mortgaging the Future?"* December 26, 2007, 3–5.

[311] USDOC, BEA, *Survey of Current Business*, October 2009, 40–43, 52–53; USDOC, BEA, *Survey of Current Business*, October 2004, 58.

[312] United Nations Educational, Scientific and Cultural Organization (UNESCO), Institute for Statistics, *Global Education Digest 2009*, 2009, 146; UNESCO, *Global Education Digest 2006*, 2006, 135.

[313] U.S. industry representative, interview by USITC staff, Washington, DC, November 12, 2009; Council of Graduate Schools (CGS), *Findings from the 2009 CGS International Graduate Admissions Survey*, November 2009, 9, 14, 22. Findings in the most recent survey of CGS member universities are consistent with the trend in previous CGS surveys indicating declining rates of growth and, most recently, accelerated declines in offers of admission to and enrollment by Indian graduate students at U.S. universities.

[314] Neelakantan, "India Struggles to Become a Destination for Foreign Students," July 10, 2009, A20.

[315] Dongaonkar and Negi, *International Students in Indian Universities, 2007–2008*, 2009, 2, 6; Indiastat, "Region/Countrywise Enrolment of Foreign Students in Indian Universities" (accessed September 1, 2009). Short-term study in India by foreign students is not included in the data.

[316] However, the Indian government has prepared legislation not yet submitted for parliamentary consideration to allow foreign universities to establish branch campuses for awarding degrees recognized in India.

[317] Neelakantan, "India Struggles to Become a Destination for Foreign Students," July 10, 2009, A20; Walters, Stapleton, and Andrews, *India's Services Sector: Unlocking Opportunity*, 2007, 57; Agarwal, "Higher Education in India," June 2006, 11. More than 130 higher education institutions in India have collaborative arrangements with institutions abroad, especially with those in the United States, Australia, and the United Kingdom, but also with universities in a wide range of developing and developed countries. Examples include a joint venture between Western International University (Apollo Group, U.S.) and the K.K. Modi Group (India); associations with the India School of Business by leading business schools at U.S. and British universities; research collaborations with Australia's Monash University and University of Melbourne; and joint-degree programs between universities in China and India that brought more than 2,500 Chinese students to Indian universities in 2009, up from 200 in 2004.

3[18] Various educational institutions' Web sites, including www.manipal.edu,
      www.imtdubai.ac.ae/index.aspx, www.bitspilani.ac.in/index.html, www.spjain.org, and
      www.diacedu.ae (accessed September 3–October 10, 2009).

[319] WTO, Council for Trade in Services, Special Session, "India: Revised Offer," August 24,
      2005.

[320] Agarwal, "Higher Education in India," June 2006, 80–81, 172–74. Examples include the
      Ministries of Health, Social Justice, Agriculture, and Law.

[321] Government of India, Ministry of Human Resource Development, *Annual Report 2007–08*,
      118; Sahasrabudhe and Muthanna, "Making Sense of Accreditation for Higher Education,"
      May 2009, 2.

[322] AICTE issues regulations on academic courses, curricula, and educational facilities, and
      approves the formation of new technical education institutions and the introduction of new
      technical courses in accordance with its norms and standards.

[323] Agarwal, "Higher Education in India," June 2006, 80–103; Kapur and Crowley, "Beyond the
      ABCs," February 2008, 73–74; Kapur and Mehta, "Mortgaging the Future?" December 26,
      2007, 7–8; Sunder, "Yash Pal Committee Report on Higher Education," June 26, 2009.

[324] Government of India, Ministry of Human Resource Development, "New Policy on Distance
      Learning in Higher Education," August 28, 2009.

[325] World Bank, "India: Country Summary of Higher Education," n.d., 12.

[326] World Bank, "India: Country Summary of Higher Education," n.d., 13. As a group,
      universities fared better, since nearly twice as many scored high as were rated low, although
      about half were scored medium.

[327] Anitha and Patwardhan, "Emerging Directions in Global Education," August 10, 2008, 304.

[328] Neelakantan, "India's Faculty Shortage Hits Elite Business Schools," December 12, 2008.

[329] Gupta, "Caste, Class, and Quality at the Indian Institutes of Technology," 2008; Neelakantan,
      "India's Faculty Shortage Hits Elite Business Schools," December 12, 2008; Neelakantan,
      "Rapid Expansion Strains Elite Indian Institutes," January 30, 2009, A20; Seshagiri, "All
      Seven IIMs Reeling under Faculty Crunch," December 10, 2008.

[330] Neelakantan, "India's Faculty Shortage Hits Elite Business Schools," December 12, 2008;
      Vishnoi, "Back in India, Academics Apply to UGC for Teaching Jobs," May 28, 2009.

[331] Mehrotra, "Indian Higher Education," Summer 2009.

[332] Patnaik, "Orissa Passes Vedanta University Bill with Amendments," July 30, 2009; Reuters,
      "Talent Building Key Challenge for India," August 11, 2009. Anil Agarwal committed $1
      billion to create Vedanta University in the State of Orissa, India. The state assembly
      approved formation of the university in July 2009. The first academic programs in the
      colleges of arts and science, engineering, and management are expected to begin in 2011,
      followed by programs in law, medicine, agriculture, bioscience, and performing arts. The
      founder's plan is to establish Vedanta University as a world-class, research-driven
      institution ultimately enrolling 100,000 students, along with a related research park and
      hospital, among other facilities.

[333] *Gazette of India*, "UGC (Minimum Standards and Procedure for Awards of M.Phil./Ph.D.
      Degrees), Regulation, 2009," July 11, 2009, 4053–54; "UGC (Minimum Qualifications
      Required for the Appointment and Career Advancement of Teachers in Universities and
      Institutions Affiliated to It) (3rd Amendment), Regulation, 2009," July 11, 2009, 4055–56.

[334] UGC, "Territorial Jurisdiction of the State Universities/State Private Universities," April 16
      and 28, 2009.

[335] World Trade Organization, Services Statistics Database: India.

[336] RBI, "A Profile of Banks 2008–09," September 9, 2009.

[337] McKinsey & Company, *Indian Banking*, November 2007, 18.

[338] McKinsey & Company, *Indian Banking*, November 2007, 16.

[339] EIU, *Country Finance: India*, July 2009, 5.

[340] The degree of government ownership in these banks varies. Some are wholly owned by the government, while others are majority state-owned with a minority share publicly traded.

[341] EIU, *Country Finance: India*, July 2009, 12.

[342] EIU, *Country Finance: India*, July 2009, 12, and EIU, *Country Finance: India*, July 2005, 10.

[343] EIU, *Country Finance: India*, July 2009, 12.

[344] EIU, *Country Finance: India*, July 2009, 14.

[345] Market share is calculated based on loan advances in fiscal year 2008. EIU, *Country Finance: India*, July 2009, 14.

[346] Mamta, "Mobiles Can Build a More Inclusive Financial System," June 1, 2009.

[347] McKinsey & Company, *Indian Banking*, November 2007, 16.

[348] Rural and cooperative banks are regulated by the RBI and state authorities, which often raises questions of responsibility for oversight and results in regulatory lapses.

[349] EIU, *Country Finance: India*, July 2009, 14.

[350] RBI, "Mobile Banking Transactions in India–Operative Guidelines for Banks," October 8, 2008.

[351] WTO Secretariat, *Trade Policy Review*, April 18, 2007, 130.

[352] EIU, *Country Finance: India*, July 2009, 9.

[353] EIU, *Country Finance: India*, July 2009, 9.

[354] Miscellaneous services include communications services; construction services; financial services; news agency services; royalties, copyrights and license fees; business services; personal, cultural and recreational services; and other services. RBI, "India's Balance of Payments Developments," *RBI Monthly Bulletin*, October 2009, 1795.

[355] Reserve Bank of India, "Indian Investment Abroad," RBI Monthly Bulletin, October 2009,1782–83.

[356] State Bank of India, "Annual Results FY 09," May 13, 2009.

[357] USDOC, BEA, *Survey of Current Business*, October 2009, 52.

[358] USDOC, BEA, *Survey of Current Business*, October 2009, 53.

[359] Data on investment in Indian depository institutions were suppressed for 2008. USDOC, BEA, *Survey of Current Business*, September 2009.

[360] Data on investment in U.S. non-depository institutions and insurance during 2006–08 were either suppressed or unavailable. USDOC, BEA, *Survey of Current Business*, September 2009.

[361] The first phase of the roadmap began in March 2005 and established rules for entry of new banks, branch expansion by existing banks, conversion of existing branches to wholly owned subsidiaries, and acquisition of shares in domestic private banks. RBI "Roadmap for the Presence of Foreign Banks Operating in India," February 28, 2005.

[362] USTR, "India," 2009, 243.

[363] McKinsey & Company, "Indian Banking," November 2007, 8.

[364] WTO, Council for Trade in Services, Special Session, "India: Revised Offer," August 24, 2005.

[365] WTO, Council for Trade in Services, Special Session, "India: Revised Offer," August 24, 2005.

[366] RBI, "Annual Policy Statement—2009–10," April 21, 2009.

[367] Government of India, Ministry of Commerce and Industry, Department of Industrial Policy and Promotion, Circular 1 of 2010: Consolidated FDI Policy, section 5.39.1.1,

http://siadipp.nic.in/policy/fdi_circular/fdi_circular_1_2010.pdf; Roy, "A Backdoor that Leads Nowhere," May 10, 2010. 368 Mattoo, Mishra, and Shingal, "Sustaining India's Services Revolution," 2004, 50–51; WTO Secretariat, *Trade Policy Review*, April 18, 2007, 125.

[369] A study from 2003 suggests the extent of potential welfare gains from further liberalization: the study estimated that a 33 percent reduction in the level of India's barriers to trade in services would yield a 0.55 percent increase in Indian GDP. The study used the computable general equilibrium model of the National Council for Applied Economic Research and the University of Michigan, which is based on the Michigan Model of World Production and Trade. Chadha et al., "Services Issues and Liberalization in the Doha Development Agenda Negotiations," 2003, 20–22 and 33.

In: India and Malaysia: Service Sector Growth   ISBN: 978-1-61470-508-6
Editors: Samir Orujov, Souta Mori   © 2012 Nova Science Publishers, Inc.

Chapter 2

AN OVERVIEW AND EXAMINATION
OF THE MALAYSIAN SERVICE SECTOR[*]

Lisa Alejandro, Jennifer Baumert Powell,
Samantha Brady, and Isaac Wohl

ABSTRACT

The service sector is a rapidly growing component of Malaysia's economy. In 2008, the last year for which data are available, it expanded 7.2 percent to $96.9 billion and employed over half of the country's workforce. Growth in the Malaysian service sector is largely a product of government policies that promote service industries, including tax benefits and investment, as well as specialization in niche service industries that cater to Islamic consumers. In April 2009, the government eliminated or eased ethnic-Malay equity requirements in 27 service industries in an effort to further increase service industries' contribution to the Malaysian economy.

The growing global competitiveness of Malaysia's service sector is reflected in steady growth in trade volumes. Malaysia's cross-border trade in services increased at an average annual rate of 15 percent to $60.6 billion from 2004 through 2008, accounting for 13 percent of total Malaysian cross-border trade and about 1 percent of global services trade in 2008. While the United States maintains a surplus in cross-border

---

[*] This is an edited, reformatted and augmented version of a United States International Trade Commission publication No. ID-21, dated November 2010.

services trade with Malaysia;[1] its imports from Malaysia in this sector grew faster than the corresponding exports from 2004 through 2008. In 2008, U.S. cross-border services exports to Malaysia totaled $2.0 billion, while services imports from Malaysia totaled $1.3 billion. Intangible intellectual property and tourism services account for the largest shares of U.S. services exports to Malaysia.

Quantitative analysis suggests that the existence of nontariff measures continues to inhibit foreign participation in Malaysian service industries. While Malaysia has made significant efforts to liberalize certain service industries, Commission staff analysis indicates that further liberalization could increase Malaysia's yearly services imports from the rest of the world by as much as $2.6 billion.

INTRODUCTION

The service sector is a large and growing component of Malaysia's expanding economy, accounting for almost 55 percent of that country's gross domestic product (GDP)[2] and approximately 13 percent of total Malaysian cross-border trade in 2008.[3] A significant part of the Malaysian government's current economic strategy is aimed at improving the competitiveness of the Malaysian service sector, with dedicated programs to encourage domestic and foreign investment in certain service industries and increase these industries' productivity.[4] Malaysia is one of Asia's key service markets, given its ties with regional partners, including members of the Association of Southeast Asian Nations (ASEAN);[5] its significant overall bilateral trade relationship with the United States;[6] its status as the site of significant U.S. foreign investment;[7] and its ongoing negotiations with the United States in pursuit of a bilateral free trade agreement (FTA).[8]

This paper is the second in a series of studies that identify and examine important characteristics and trends affecting developing-country markets for services.[9] The paper begins with an overview of the Malaysian service sector, including data and analysis on the size and growth of that country's service sector and a discussion of factors affecting supply and demand in the Malaysian services market. Following the overview, the paper focuses on factors affecting Malaysia's position in the global service market, Malaysian service trade with the world, and the potential effect of liberalization in the Malaysian service sector. This paper also provides overviews and analyses of three discrete Malaysian service industries which have experienced particularly notable growth or development in recent years, including the banking, healthcare, and logistic services industries.

OVERVIEW OF THE MALAYSIAN SERVICE SECTOR

Strong performance in Malaysia's service sector[10] has been the key to recent growth in that country's economy. According to data reported by Treasury Malaysia, output in Malaysia's service sector increased by 9.6 percent in 2007 and by 7.2 percent in 2008, surpassing growth in other sectors of the economy and accounting for a significant share of the growth in Malaysia's total GDP during those respective years—4.5 percent in 2007 and 5.4 percent in 2008.[11] Growth in the Malaysian services market was comparable to that posted in other southeast Asian service markets in 2008, including Vietnam and Indonesia (6.1 percent each); the Philippines (3.8 percent); Thailand (2.6 percent); and Singapore (1.1 percent).[12]

Services industries also account for the largest share of Malaysian employment. Employment in the Malaysian service sector grew at an average annual rate of 3.5 percent between 2004 and 2008, reaching 6.0 million workers, or 52 percent of total employment in 2008.[13] By comparison, total employment in Malaysia grew at an average annual rate of 2.6 percent during this period, reaching 11.6 million workers in 2008.[14]

According to Treasury Malaysia, large private industries within the Malaysian service sector include wholesale and retail trade services and finance and insurance services, which respectively accounted for 24 percent and 21 percent of Malaysian service GDP in 2008 (figure 1).[15] In that year, the fastest-growing service industries were government services and the wholesale and retail trade industry, which grew by 11.1 percent and 9.8 percent, respectively.[16] Malaysia's tourism industry—which includes restaurant and accommodation services, among other activities—also experienced significant growth in recent years, partly due to government efforts to support this industry through the hosting of sports events and international conventions.[17]

Government policies, including past and present bumiputra, or ethnic Malay, preferences,[18] have produced a service sector that is characterized by a large number of small and medium-sized enterprises (SMEs).[19] Malaysia's most recent *SME Annual Report* indicated that over 99 percent of all Malaysian companies were SMEs, and 474,706 (or almost 87 percent) of

Malaysia's SMEs were service sector enterprises.[20] The Malaysian government encourages lending to SMEs with the aim of boosting domestic investment and growth and reducing dependence on large companies.[21]

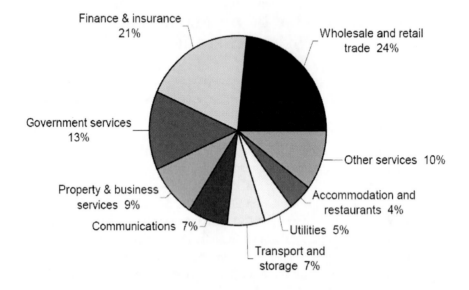

Total service sector GDP = $96.9 billion

Source: Treasury Malaysia, Economic Reports 2009/2010 , 2010, table 2.3.
Note: Values are estimated.

Figure 1. Malaysia: Service sectors as a percentage of GDP, 2008.

One financial assistance program gives grants to service sector SMEs for expenses such as start-up costs, certification and quality management systems, and advertising and promotion. A firm must be at least 60 percent Malaysian owned in order to qualify for this grant.[22] In 2008, the Malaysian government also began taking measures designed to help SMEs specifically or, in some cases, all Malaysian businesses, weather the global economic downturn.[23] A recent survey indicated that 73 percent of service sector SMEs were affected by the downturn, with some firms in the retail/food and beverage and construction segments reporting that the downturn had a severe effect on their business.[24]

Demand

Government policies have helped support the demand for services in Malaysia. Under the Ninth Malaysia Plan,[25] the Malaysian government has increased its investment in physical infrastructure, with particular emphasis on expanding its transport and container port infrastructure. Through this effort, Malaysia has sought to become a regional hub for air transport and the preferred transshipment point for the Southeast Asian region.[26] These policies will likely increase demand for construction, engineering, financial, airport, travel and tourism services, and other services related to the development and operation of transport infrastructure. The Malaysian government also aims to promote manufacturing-related services such as research and development (R&D), product design, and central utility supply and cold chain storage for the food processing industry.[27] The government hopes that these initiatives will help lengthen the country's value chain and thus increase demand for Malaysian goods and services.

Growth in disposable incomes and spending power in Asia may also increase demand for services in Malaysia, particularly in industries related to tourism such as retailing, hotels, and restaurants. Particularly rapid growth in exports of Malaysian tourism services to neighboring Asian economies[28] are attributed to recent increases in personal disposable income in these countries.[29]

Supply

Several factors affect services provision in Malaysia; two major factors are government intervention and the composition of the Malaysian workforce. The supply of services is encouraged by Malaysian government policies promoting service sector investment, including tax incentives and policies liberalizing foreign equity participation and the entry of foreign employees.[30] Malaysia's Third Industrial Master Plan (IMP3), which covers the period 2006–20, contains provisions intended to position Malaysia as a regional center for selected service industries, especially real estate, transport, telecommunications, information technology, and accommodations and tourism.[31] In 2007, domestic and foreign service sector investments totaled approximately $15 billion,[32] far surpassing the IMP3's annual investment target of $13.3 billion.[33] The Malaysian government also seeks to grow certain niche industry segments—specifically, Islamic banking, halal[34] food logistics, conference services, and medical tourism—in which the country has a competitive advantage due to its geographic location and culturally diverse population.

However, service supply in Malaysia has been hindered by persistent labor shortages throughout the past 10 years. As a result, a significant portion of the Malaysian workforce comes from foreign countries, particularly from Indonesia. An estimated 1.8 million legal and 500,000 illegal foreign workers were employed in Malaysia in 2006,[35] which is significant considering that Malaysia's economy employs slightly more than 11 million people.[36] These foreign workers are an integral part of the Malaysian economy, making up most of the construction, plantation, manufacturing, and household labor forces in the country. At the same time, Malaysia is experiencing the emigration of its skilled workers, with English-speaking workers being in particularly high demand in India, China, the Middle East, and the United States. Such emigration may undermine Malaysia's efforts to develop its service sector and become a regional and world hub for services.[37]

Until recently, another factor that likely impeded the supply of services in Malaysia was a government commitment to improve the economic status of the ethnic Malay majority, known as the bumiputra.[38] Bumiputra policy was intended to rebalance the social and economic status of ethnic Malays. In 1997, Malaysia exempted its manufacturing industries from bumiputra preferences. As a result, the service sector was seen as a particularly important market segment for the continued economic and social advancement of the bumiputra in Malaysia, and service liberalization that would affect bumiputra preferences was politically sensitive.[39] Under these preferences, the government required that both foreign and domestic firms in the service sector take on bumiputra partners and have at least 30 percent bumiputra equity.[40] These equity requirements existed for firms in the financial, business and professional, telecommunications, express delivery, and energy distribution industries,[41] among others, and exceptions to the policy were decided case-by-case.[42] In part as a result of these policies, bumiputra participation in the Malaysian service sector is particularly significant in professional services. In 2006, bumiputra accounted for 46,589 (39.6 percent) of 117,652 registered Malaysian professionals, including, for example, 25,748 engineers, 5,700 doctors, and 5,002 lawyers.[43]

In April 2009, the government eliminated or eased bumiputra equity requirements in 27 service industries, including healthcare, transportation, and tourism, among others.[44] This was done in an effort to further increase services industries' contribution to the overall Malaysian economy, in part by loosening the conditions of foreign investment.[45] Among remaining restrictions, those on financial services are the most significant.

PARTICIPATION IN THE GLOBAL SERVICES MARKET

Malaysian Services Trade with the World

Malaysian services trade has registered steady growth in recent years. In 2008, Malaysia's services exports and imports totaled $30.3 billion each, accounting for approximately 13 percent of total Malaysian cross-border trade volume. From 2004 through 2008, growth in exports outpaced growth in imports in the sector, 15 percent to 12 percent. Moreover, total Malaysian cross-border services trade (15 percent) grew slightly faster than global services trade (14 percent) from 2004 through 2008. Malaysian cross-border services trade comprises about 1 percent of global services trade.

International Monetary Fund (IMF) data on services trade indicate that travel[46] accounted for over 50 percent of Malaysian services exports in 2008 (figure 2). The Malaysian travel sector is globally competitive, in part due to government programs such as the Ninth Malaysia Plan and the Third Industrial Master Plan, as discussed above. In 2008, travel was followed by other business services[47] and passenger air transport, which accounted for over 13 percent and 11 percent of total service exports, respectively.[48] Malaysian exports of air passenger transport services rose relatively quickly from 2004 through 2008, increasing at an average annual rate of 35 percent.

In 2008, sea freight transport accounted for the largest share (32 percent) of total Malaysian services imports (figure 3).[49] From 2004 to 2008, computer and information services registered particularly rapid average annual growth (29 percent), followed by construction services (28 percent), and travel services (21 percent) industries.[50]

U.S.-Malaysia Services Trade

U.S. Department of Commerce (USDOC) Bureau of Economic Analysis (BEA) data indicate that the United States maintains a surplus in cross-border services trade with Malaysia.[51] In 2008, U.S. cross-border services exports to

Malaysia totaled $2.0 billion, while services imports from Malaysia totaled $1.3 billion.

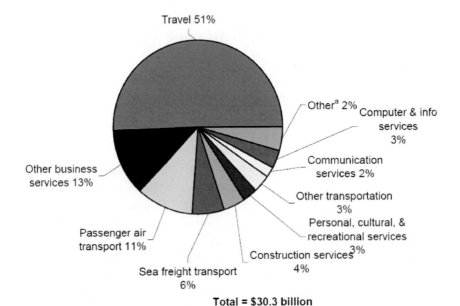

Travel 51%

Other[a] 2%

Computer & info services 3%

Communication services 2%

Other transportation 3%

Personal, cultural, & recreational services 3%

Construction services 4%

Sea freight transport 6%

Passenger air transport 11%

Other business services 13%

Total = $30.3 billion

Source: International Monetary Fund, Balance of Payments, 2010.

[a]'Other' includes insurance services ($371 million), government services not included elsewhere ($38 million), financial services ($87 million), and royalties and license fees ($199 million).

Figure 2. Malaysia: Services exports, 2008.

However, U.S. imports grew more quickly than exports from 2004 through 2008, with imports increasing at an average annual rate of 20 percent, while exports grew at a rate of 13 percent.

According to data reported by BEA, the largest component of U.S. services exports to Malaysia is intangible intellectual property, which accounted for $247 million, or 13 percent, of service exports in 2008 (figure 4). Exports of intangible intellectual property generate royalties and license fees. The majority (56 percent) of royalty and license fees exports reflect trade with unaffiliated firms, while the remainder reflects trade between U.S. parent firms and their Malaysian affiliates. General-use computer software accounted for the largest share (39 percent) of royalties and license fees collected from Malaysia, followed by license fees for industrial processes (24 percent). The second-largest component of U.S. cross-border services exports to Malaysia is tourism services, which made up 10 percent of the total in 2008.

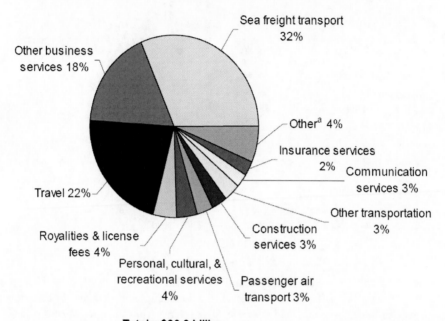

Sea freight transport 32%

Other business services 18%

Other[a] 4%

Insurance services 2% Communication services 3%

Travel 22%

Other transportation 3%

Construction services 3%

Royalities & license fees 4%

Personal, cultural, & recreational services 4%

Passenger air transport 3%

Total = $30.3 billion

Source: International Monetary Fund, Balance of Payments, 2010.
[a] Other services include computer & information services, government services not included elsewhere, and financial services.

Figure 3. Malaysia: Services imports, 2008.

By a large margin, research and development services were the largest component of U.S. services imports from Malaysia, accounting for $300 million, or 24 percent of total U.S. services imports from Malaysia in 2008 (figure 5). Next in importance were tourism services, which accounted for 11 percent of U.S. services imports from Malaysia in 2008.

While data on affiliate transactions between the United States and Malaysia are very limited, such transactions seem to have risen substantially during the past decade. In 2007, the most recent year for which data are available,52 services supplied to Malaysians by U.S.-owned affiliates totaled $3.7 billion. The 2006–07 increase of 31 percent was 10 percent more than the average growth rate for the 2004–07 period. Services supplied to U.S. persons from Malaysian-owned affiliates totaled $422 million, an increase of 16 percent from the previous year.[53]

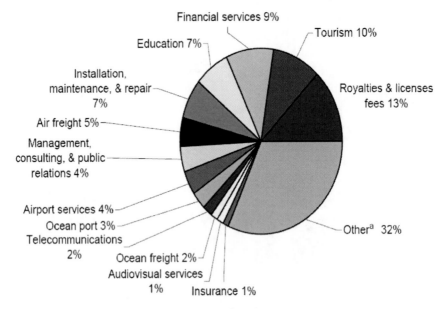

Total = $2.0 billion

Source: USDOC, BEA, Survey of Current Business 89, no. 10, 48–59.

[a] "Other" includes R&D and testing services; advertising; computer and information services; legal services and operational leasing; architecture, engineering, and construction services; and other services not included elsewhere.

Figure 4. Malaysia: U.S. cross-border exports of private services to Malaysia, 2008.

BARRIERS TO FOREIGN PARTICIPATION IN THE MALAYSIAN SERVICES SECTOR

Under the World Trade Organization (WTO) General Agreement on Trade in Services (GATS), Malaysia scheduled a certain number of commitments on the foreign provision of services, but retained a large degree of freedom to restrict services trade pursuant to development goals.

For instance, it made no commitments to grant foreigners licenses in banking, insurance, or telecommunications or to permit foreigners to provide education, environmental, or distribution services through commercial presence (mode 3).[54] Malaysia also restricted aggregate foreign equity and holdings in any Malaysian corporation to 30 percent and further stipulated that bumiputras must control 30 percent of all firms in certain subsectors.

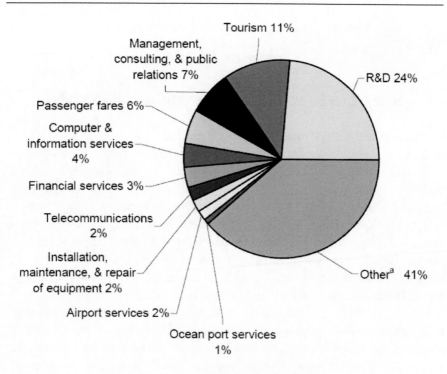

Total = $1.3 billion

Source: USDOC, BEA, Survey of Current Business 89, no. 10, 48–59.

[a]'Other' includes royalties and license fees; education; advertising; legal services; insurance services; air freight services; operational leasing; construction, architectural and engineering services; and other services not included elsewhere.

Figure 5. Malaysia: U.S. cross-border imports of private services from Malaysia, 2008.

Malaysia's most recent publicly available services offer, dated December 2005, retains these ownership limitations.

Since 2005, however, Malaysia has adopted policies under its Ninth Master Plan (2006- 2010) to further open its services sector to foreign investment. As noted, in April 2009, the Malaysian government removed bumiputra equity requirements in 27 service sectors, including healthcare and transportation services. In addition, the government eased foreign investment restrictions in financial services (see section on banking), and established new agencies to facilitate the approval of applications for foreign investment in the services sector.[55] Malaysia hopes that strengthening its domestic service suppliers through foreign investment will better prepare them to compete on a global scale, enabling the country to improve its services commitments under the GATS.[56]

SERVICES LIBERALIZATION THROUGH ASEAN

Though a signatory to the GATS and several existing or potential FTAs, Malaysia has principally liberalized its services trade through ASEAN. Along with other ASEAN members, Malaysia aims to establish an ASEAN Economic Community by 2020. To achieve this goal, member countries have been liberalizing service markets beyond their GATS commitments, which largely codified existing barriers. These efforts stem from the 1995 ASEAN Framework Agreement on Services, which brought about three rounds of service negotiations and four sets of commitments through a "Minus X" formula that enables two or more ASEAN countries to proceed with service sector liberalization without extending concessions to nonparticipating countries.[57] These liberalization packages have covered construction, telecommunications, business services, financial services, air and maritime transport, and tourism, providing member countries with preferential access in the employment of professionals and the establishment of commercial affiliates.[58] Member countries have also been negotiating a Strategic Plan of Customs Development, as well as mutual recognition arrangements for qualifications in professional services. Malaysian services liberalization under ASEAN includes member-countries' exemption from its local-content requirements on advertising services.[59]

Potential Effects of Additional Liberalization

The Commission staff has performed econometric analysis using gravity models to evaluate the potential effects of further liberalization on Malaysia's cross-border imports of services. Gravity models examine the relationship between certain variables—such as economic size, distance, and other potential sources of "trade resistance"[60]—and the volume of trade between two countries. Tinbergen developed the basic gravity model nearly 50 years ago,[61] and an extensive literature of gravity model-based studies has emerged in the decades since. While gravity models have been used to analyze trade in goods far more often than trade in services, authors such as Grünfeld and Moxnes[62] and Kimura and Lee[63] have demonstrated their usefulness for analyzing services trade.

The starting point for our models is the "standard"[64] gravity equation:

$$lnIM_{ij} = \beta_1 + \beta_2 lnY_i + \beta_3 lnY_j + \beta_4 ln D_{ij} + \varepsilon_{ij}$$

where $_{IMij}$ is country i's imports from country j; Y_i and Y_j are the GDP of country i and j, respectively; [65] D_{ij} is the distance from country i to country j; and $_{\varepsilon ij}$ is the error term. The log-log specification makes it easier to analyze the elasticity of trade volumes with respect to the trading partners' GDP and the distance between them.

Gravity studies have sought to account for a variety of additional factors influencing the volume of trade. Following Kimura and Lee, we include dummy variables for adjacency and common language.[66] The adjacency variable traditionally controls for country pairs that share a border; we extend this to include country pairs facing each other across a small sea. The intuition is that direct neighbors should trade more because they face lower transaction costs. The common-language variable captures the idea that countries that share a language—and the broader cultural affinities associated with the use of that language—may face lower costs to trade.

Nontariff measures (NTMs) may also affect flows of trade in services (unlike goods, services are virtually never subject to tariffs). Grünfeld and Moxnes, Kimura and Lee, and Walsh[67] use a variety of measures in their models in order to capture the effects of NTMs on services trade. [68] We use a new measure: an index of restrictions on inward FDI in services developed by Golub.[69]

Measures of FDI restrictions are useful proxies for barriers to cross-border trade in services because empirical analyses strongly suggest that in the case of services, FDI facilitates trade, while restrictions on FDI inhibit trade.[70] For example, Fillat-Castejón, Francois, and Wörz examine the extent to which FDI inflows and cross-border imports of services are complements or substitutes. They find strong evidence of a complementary effect of FDI on services imports, in both the short and the long run. Furthermore, they find that barriers to foreign ownership (i.e., FDI) have a significant, negative effect on cross-border imports of services.[71] These findings buttress those of Grünfeld and Moxnes, who create gravity models that use service exports and the stock of outward FDI in services as dependent variables. They test for complementarity by regressing the residuals from the FDI model on the residuals from the exports model, and find a positive and highly significant relationship, meaning that services exports and investment move in tandem.[72]

Golub's index has a number of advantages over alternative indices: it is specific to services; it measures "applied" barriers (as opposed to those "bound" in WTO commitments); and it covers more countries (73) and industries (eight) than other measures of applied services NTMs. Golub scores the countries on a scale of 0 (least restrictive) to 1 (most restrictive), accounting for regulations on foreign ownership and screening and approval rules, as well as operational restrictions for the period 2004–05 (table 1).

Table 1. FDI Restriction Scoring Method

Foreign Ownership	
No foreign equity allowed	1
1–19% foreign equity allowed	0.6
20–34% foreign equity allowed	0.5
35–49% foreign equity allowed	0.4
50–74% foreign equity allowed	0.2
75–99% foreign equity allowed	0.1
Screening and approval	
Investor must show economic benefits	0.2
Approval unless contrary to national interest	0.1
Notification (pre- or post-establishment)	0.05
Operational Restrictions	
Board of directors/managers majority must be nationals	0.1
Duration of work permit for expatriates less than one	0.1
one to two years	0.05
three to four years	0.025
Other operational restrictions	up to 0.1
Total (capped at 1.0)	*Between 0 and 1*

Source: Golub, "Openness to Foreign Direct Investment in Services," 2009.

He assesses barriers in eight industries: business services, telecommunications, construction, distribution, electricity, financial services, tourism, and travel. Golub uses an average of FDI and trade weights to generate an index score for overall restrictions on services FDI for each country.

Our model also includes a remoteness variable to control for the effects of "relative distance"; countries that are close to each other but far from the rest of the world can be expected to trade more with each other than the rest of the world. We define remoteness (REM) as

$$REM_i = \Sigma d_{im}/y_m$$

where dim is the distance from country i to all trade partners, and y_m is the GDP of the trading partners of country i.[73]

We estimate our model two ways: first, with random effects[74] using year dummies from 2000 to 2006, and secondly, with ordinary least squares (OLS) for 2004:

1. $lnIM_{jit} = \beta_1 + \beta_2\ lnY_{it} + \beta_3\ lnY_{jt} + \beta_4\ lnD_{ijt} + \beta_5\ A_{ij} + \beta_6\ CL_{ij} + \beta_7$
    $SFDIR_{ij} + \beta_8 lnREM_{it} + \beta_9 lnREM_{jt} + \beta_{10}Y01 + \beta_{11}Y02 + \beta_{12}Y03 +$
    $\beta_{13}Y04 + \beta_{14}Y05 + \beta_{15}Y06 + \varepsilon_{ij}$
2. $lnIM_{ji} = \beta_1 + \beta_2\ lnY_i + \beta_3\ lnY_j + \beta_4\ lnD_{ij} + \beta_5\ A_{ij} + \beta_6\ CL_{ij} + \beta_7\ SFDIR_{ij} +$
    $\beta_8 lnREM_i + \beta_9 lnREM_j + \varepsilon_{ij}$

where A_{ij} and CL_{ij} are adjacency and common language dummies; $SFDIR_{ij}$ is the overall services FDI restrictiveness index; REM is remoteness of country i and country j, respectively; and $Y01$– $Y06$ are year dummies in the random effects model.[75] We use 2004 data for the OLS model because it is one of the two years for which the $SFDIR$ data were collected. The bilateral service imports data are taken from the Organisation for Economic Co-operation and Development's (OECD) Statistics on International Trade in Services, which contains 26 of the 31 OECD countries and Russia as exporters, along with 70 importing countries.[76] The World Bank's World Development Indicators (WDI) is the source for GDP, measured in 2000 constant U.S. dollars. Distance, adjacency, and common language are calculated by the Centre d'Etudes Prospectives et d'Informations Internationales.

In both specifications, GDP is strongly and positively associated with exports, while distance is strongly and negatively associated with trade, as expected. Remoteness has a positive effect in the panel regression, with increased significance over the OLS model. This result suggests that the random effects model is a more efficient estimator than the OLS model. Adjacency has a slightly positive but insignificant effect. This may be due to the fact that there are very few country pairs in the dataset which are adjacent; it could also suggest that sharing a border is less important for trade in services than trade in goods. The common language variable has a highly positive and significant effect on trade. The adjusted R-squared values for the random effects and OLS model are .737 and .700, respectively, meaning that the model explains about 70 percent of the variation in cross-border imports of services (table 2).

The services FDI restrictiveness index has a substantial explanatory effect. The coefficient is approximately −1.3 in both models, and is significant at the 5 percent and 1 percent level for the OLS and random effects model, respectively. The magnitude of the services FDI restrictiveness index indicates that a decrease of 0.01 in a country's restrictiveness score is associated with a 1.3 percent increase in imports of services into that country.

Potential Effects of Future Liberalization in Malaysia

Malaysia's services FDI restrictiveness index score is 0.53. Using the random effects model, we can examine the possible effects of further FDI liberalization for Malaysia. If Malaysia reduced FDI restrictions to the mean (0.24), cross-border imports by Malaysia could be expected to increase by approximately 39.8 percent, ceteris paribus.[77] If Malaysia liberalized to the minimum restrictiveness (0.04), cross-border imports by Malaysia could be expected to increase by approximately 67.3 percent (table 3). In 2005, Malaysia imported approximately $3.8 billion of services from 21 countries in the model.

Results

The services FDI restrictiveness index is right skewed, meaning that most countries in the dataset are relatively open (appendix A, tables A.1 and A.2). The most restrictive score is only 67 percent of the maximum possible. The 2004 data are very similar overall to the panel data.

The variables are highly correlated in a few instances, but not so broadly as to undermine the model (tables A.3 and A.4).

Liberalizing Malaysia's services FDI restrictiveness index to the mean score would correlate with an increase in imports to approximately $5.3 billion, and liberalization to the minimum score would correlate with an increase in imports to $6.4 billion.

Table 2. Gravity model: Dependent variable – *ln* (services imports)

	Random effects	OLS
Service FDI restrictiveness	-1.373‡	-1.314†
	(-3.85)	(-3.41)
ln (importer's GDP)	0.914‡	0.850 ‡
	(29.62)	(25.73)
ln (exporter's GDP)	1.809‡	0.987 ‡
	(16.64)	(25.51)
ln (distance)	-1.214‡	-0.996‡
	(-16.9)	(-12.44)
ln (importer's remoteness)	0.186 †	0.012
	(2.03)	(0.12)
ln (exporter's remoteness)	0.746‡	0.121
	(6.94)	(1.43)
Adjacency	0.096	0.272
	(0.61)	(1.26)
Common language	1.177‡	1.163‡
	(7.3)	(6.84)
Constant	-45.664‡	-33.396‡
	(-19.66)	(-14.46)
Year01	-0.008	
	(-0.25)	
Year02	0.037	
	(1.25)	
Year03	0.238‡	
	(7.84)	
Year04	0.451 ‡	
	(14.57)	
Year05	0.509‡	
	(15.67)	
Year06	0.349‡	
	(4.56)	
Number of observations	4455	858
Overall/adjusted R-squared	0.737	0.700

‡ 1 percent level of significance.
† 5 percent level of significance.
* 10 percent level of significance.

Table 3. Malaysia Liberalization Results

Malaysia SFDIR		Mean SFDIR	Min. SFDIR	Coefficient	Liberalized to average	Liberalized to miinimum
Random effects	0.53	0.24	0.04	-1.37	39.82%	67.28%
OLS	0.53	0.24	0.04	-1.31	38.11%	64.39%

SECTOR INDUSTRY PROFILES

Banking

Overview

Financial services play a significant and increasing role in the Malaysian economy. In 2007, financial services accounted for 16 percent of Malaysia's gross national product, making it the largest contributor among the service industries.[78] Assets in the banking system—including commercial banks, merchant banks, and finance companies—totaled approximately $420 billion in March 2010, a 76 percent increase over 2005 levels.[79] In 2009, employment in the finance, insurance, real estate, and business services industries[80] was estimated at 814,100, accounting for 7 percent of overall employment. This figure reflects a 11 percent increase over 2005 levels.[81]

Government Policies and Sector Reform

Under the Financial Sector Master Plan (Plan), which began implementation in 2001, the Malaysian government has placed a strong emphasis on banking consolidation and reform. The Plan, which guides Malaysian banks through 2010, was designed to strengthen domestic financial institutions in order to increase the financial sector's contribution to economic growth and to prepare domestic firms for increased competition from foreign banks.[82] In phase I, the Plan concentrated on consolidating the domestic market through mergers and acquisitions. Phase II was designed to lift restrictions on incumbent foreign banks in order to promote competition. During phase III, the government plans to consider opening the market to new foreign firms.[83] The consolidation in phase I was undertaken swiftly, but it is unclear when the provisions outlined in the subsequent phases will be implemented.

Another stated objective of the Plan is to fashion Malaysia into a global hub for Islamic banking. Such banks offer specially designed products that comply with Islamic—or Sharia—law, which prohibits charging interest. The Plan aims for Islamic banking assets to account for 20 percent of total banking assets by 2010, and the government has offered incentives intended to advance the Islamic finance segment of the financial service industry.[84] This aggressive approach to developing Islamic banking has led to increases in both the supply of and demand for such services. By the end of September 2009, Islamic banking assets accounted for 16 percent of total banking sector assets, with deposits to Islamic banks growing by 20 percent over the previous year and financing increasing by 22 percent.[85]

Malaysia's solid economic growth in recent years has led to rising incomes among individuals and businesses, creating a need for safer and more sophisticated financial services. The Malaysian government has sought to boost public confidence in its financial sector by introducing new consumer protection measures that encourage Malaysians to entrust their money to the formal financial service industry. Most significantly, in 2005, the Malaysia Deposit Insurance Corporation was established to insure deposits up to RM60,000 (approximately $18,575).[86]

Malaysia's domestic banking firms are well protected from foreign competition by government regulations specifically designed to this end. New foreign firms are limited to a 49 percent equity stake in investment banks and a 30 percent stake in commercial banks.[87] Foreign banks operating in Malaysia must be locally incorporated and maintain all-Malaysian boards of directors. All banks are required to conduct back-office and data activities in the country, putting an extra cost burden on foreign banks. In addition, foreign firms are not permitted to connect their ATM machines to the domestic network. To circumvent that limitation, four foreign banks—Standard Chartered, HSBC, OverseaChinese Banking Corp, and United Overseas Bank—collaborated in 2006 to establish their own shared network, allowing their customers to use any of the 300 ATMs operated by those banks.[88]

The Malaysian banking industry has already undergone some consolidation, and it is likely to consolidate further. Malaysia has 39 commercial banks, including 9 domestically owned, 13 foreign owned but locally incorporated, and 17 Islamic banks.[89] Domestic firms dominate the sector—accounting for 80 percent of total banking assets in May 2008[90]—and offer a wide range of banking services, including commercial, retail, and investment services, as well as insurance, property management, and fund management. Starting in 1999, the Malaysian government began consolidating domestically-owned banks. This effort was designed to create larger domestic banks that would be better able to withstand competition from foreign firms entering the market. As a result, 58 banks were consolidated into 9 domestic banking groups, each of which operates a commercial firm as well as an investment and/or an Islamic bank. The three largest domestic banking groups in Malaysia are the Maybank Group, BumiputraCommerce Holdings Group, and the Public Banking Group, which collectively hold a 57 percent share of the market.[91] The government has stated that it aims to further consolidate domestic banks into 3 or 4 firms, but it remains unclear when that might occur.

Growth in the Banking Sector

Malaysia's foreign banking sector has grown rapidly despite substantial restrictions on market entry and operations. There are 13 foreign banks operating in Malaysia, collectively accounting for $86 billion, or 20 percent, of the commercial banking sector's total assets.[92] This represents a 122 percent gain in foreign bank assets since 2005.[93] The five most prominent foreign banks operating in Malaysia—HSBC (UK), OverseaChinese Banking Corp (Singapore), Standard Chartered (UK), Citibank (U.S.), and United Overseas Bank (Singapore)—collectively accounted for 18 percent of the Malaysian banking market in July 2009.[94] All 13 foreign banks that currently operate in Malaysia are permitted to offer a full range of commercial and retail banking services, though only the top 5 banks have significant branch networks and retail and commercial operations. The remaining banks tend to focus on more specialized market segments, such as providing services to multinational companies or trade financing. In 2005, the central bank announced that existing foreign banks could each open four new branches during the following year, with one in an urban commercial market, two in semiurban centers, and one in a rural area.[95] Despite this small increase in the permitted number of branches, foreign firms continue to be at a disadvantage relative to their domestic counterparts because their branching networks are restricted, limiting their access to retail deposits—a vital and inexpensive source of capital for banks.

Islamic banks have achieved substantial growth principally due to development of products comparable to those of conventional banks, though government policies have lent a helping hand. These banks operate according to Sharia (Islamic) law, which prohibits the payment or collection of interest and encourages profit and loss sharing. In order to accommodate these basic principles, Islamic banks offer alternative financial vehicles. For example, in lieu of traditional secured loans for real estate, automobiles, etc., that charge the borrower interest, Islamic banks offer arrangements such as murabaha financing, whereby the bank purchases the asset and then sells it to the borrower at an agreed-upon markup.[96] Such markups typically reflect conventional interest rates. As Islamic banks cannot pay interest on deposits, funds are either deposited on a fiduciary basis or placed into investment account funds which the bank manages, sharing profits and losses with the depositor.[97] In January 2010, Islamic banks accounted for $70 billion, or 18 percent, of total commercial banking assets in Malaysia, representing a 79 percent increase over December 2006 levels.[98] Because Malaysia has placed a priority on becoming a global hub for Islamic banking—and thus has devoted the majority of its recent financial services liberalization efforts to that industry segment—it is likely that future growth in this area will outpace that of conventional banks.

Trade and Investment

While official data on Malaysian exports of financial services are not available, industry data suggest that such exports are small but growing. Only three of Malaysia's nine commercial banking groups conduct significant operations in foreign markets. The Maybank Group holds the greatest share of foreign assets, totaling $30.9 billion in 2009; these represented 34 percent of the firm's total assets.[99] Most of these assets are concentrated in the Singaporean market, where the bank has focused its foreign operations. Bumiputra-Commerce Holdings Group and the Public Banking Group each conduct overseas operations as well, but on a smaller scale. In 2008, the BumiputraCommerce Holdings group had $6.4 billion in foreign assets: these were located mainly in Indonesia, with smaller operations in Singapore, the United Kingdom, Hong Kong, and Mauritius. The firm's operations in those countries primarily focus on corporate lending and borrowing, and securities transactions.[100] The Public Banking Group had the smallest volume of assets in foreign markets in 2009, totaling $6.2 billion, which were dispersed among a half-dozen Asian countries.[101] These figures represent growth rates of between 74 and 114 percent from 2006 levels, indicating the banks' increasing interest in expanding beyond the domestic market. Malaysia's total imports of financial services— including banking, securities, and insurance services— rose by 69 percent from 2006 to 2007, the latest years for which data are available, though it is unclear which subsector(s) were responsible for the increase.[102]

Cross-border trade in financial services between Malaysia and the United States is minimal, and is likely concentrated in the trade financing segment. Financial service exports to Malaysia totaled $183 million in 2008, representing a 48 percent increase over the preceding year.[103] Imports of financial services from Malaysia totaled $41 million in 2008, a 9 percent decrease from 2007 levels but an 18 percent increase since 2002.[104] The general increases in both imports and exports likely reflect rising levels of trade in goods between the two countries. Official data on transactions by Malaysian financial service affiliates in the United States and U.S. financial service affiliates in Malaysia are not available.

Malaysia's Banking Commitments under the GATS

In its revised GATS offer, dated December 2005, Malaysia committed to partial liberalization of the banking sector by increasing the ceiling on foreign equity investment in certain financial institutions to 49 percent. However, Malaysia's offer retained some restrictions on the operation of foreign banks included in its 1994 schedule of commitments. For instance, foreign financial institutions wishing to lend to local consumers must do so in conjunction with Malaysian banks. In addition, foreign equity participation in institutions that provide money and foreign exchange broking services is limited to 30 percent. Malaysia's offer also maintained mode 4 (presence of natural persons) restrictions in certain banking subsectors. These restrictions limit the number of foreign personnel employed in locally established offices of foreign banks.[105]

According to the WTO's most recent review of Malaysia's trade policies, the Malaysian government plans or has implemented new measures to open foreign participation in its banking sector beyond what is stated in the country's 2005 GATS offer. Such measures, which are outlined in Malaysia's Financial Sector Master Plan, include raising foreign equity ceilings in Malaysian banks and allowing locally incorporated foreign banks to establish branches for microfinance. In April 2009, the Malaysian government increased foreign equity limitations for both Islamic banks and investment banks from 49 percent to 70 percent.[106] In addition, the government issued new licenses to foreign entities wishing to establish either Islamic banks or commercial banks, and planned to issue more licenses in 2010. Finally, the government permitted locally incorporated foreign commercial banks to establish up to 10 microfinance branches, with four additional new branches permitted in 2010.[107]

Healthcare Services

Overview

The Malaysian healthcare service market is a dual system composed of public and private institutions.[108] Government-subsidized public institutions provide primary, secondary, and tertiary care at little or no cost to patients, and ensure that care is provided in rural areas and to the needy.[109] Private institutions cater to an increasingly affluent patient population, generally in urban areas, and are frequently equipped with the latest medical technology.[110] In 2008, the public sector accounted for 143 hospitals with a total of 41,249 beds, while the private sector accounted for 243 hospitals with 12,137 beds.[111] The majority of Malaysian healthcare professionals are employed in the public healthcare sector—60 percent of doctors and 71 percent of nurses in 2008.[112]

The Malaysian healthcare industry has grown in recent years, largely driven by the private sector. Total expenditure on health services increased at an average annual rate of 10.7 percent from 2004 through 2008, accounting for 4.3 percent of GDP in 2008.[113] Overall, private spending on healthcare services increased at an average annual rate of 13.9 percent between 2004 and 2008, compared to 7.3 percent for government, or public, expenditure on health.[114] Although risk-pooling and prepaid health plans (insurance) are growing in popularity, 73.2 percent of private expenditures on health in 2008 comprised out-of-pocket payments by private households.[115]

Government Policies and Sector Reform

Government policy has actively promoted growth in Malaysia's healthcare industry, especially that of private healthcare providers. The Malaysian government is the country's primary healthcare provider, and remains highly influential in both the public and private healthcare markets, contributing to the development of healthcare infrastructure in both sectors. Under the Ninth Malaysia Plan, the government increased allocations to the public sector, with RM1.3 billion ($354 million) earmarked for the construction of new hospitals and RM4.3 billion ($1.2 billion) for upgrading and renovating existing public facilities.[116] The government also enacted policies supporting the private sector, in an effort to shift the provision of healthcare services to the private market.[117] These changes include privatization of nonclinical services and the creation of tax incentives for construction, training, equipment, and other healthcare expenses.[118] The government also offers tax deductions for Malaysian consumers to offset out-of-pocket medical expenses and insurance costs. Tax deductions are allowed up to RM500 ($146) for a complete medical examination; RM3,000 ($877) for personal medical insurance premiums; RM5,000 ($1,462) for medical expenses for serious diseases; and an additional RM5,000 ($1,462) for medical expenses for parents.[119]

Malaysia's economic development and population growth have also stimulated growth in the private healthcare sector, as institutions are established to meet the increasing demands of a growing, increasingly prosperous workforce and urban population.[120] The expansion of healthcare financing options, particularly private or employer-sponsored health insurance, also increased the purchasing power of consumers, further motivating them to seek care in the private sector.[121] The number of private facilities has expanded rapidly in recent years in response to growing demand.[122] From 2003 through 2007, the number of establishments in Malaysia's private healthcare sector increased 30 percent from 3,768 to approximately 4,898.[123]

As in other developing countries, a "brain drain" is causing a labor shortage in Malaysia's healthcare system, as many medical professionals leave the country for positions with higher pay or better working conditions. Malaysia has 7 physicians per 10,000 people compared to 26 physicians per 10,000 people in the United States. Malaysia's low physician-to-patient ratio is largely the result of outward migration by healthcare workers, often to other Islamic countries such as Singapore and Saudi Arabia. 124 Further, regulations restricting pay rates and the procurement of equipment in the public sector have led many healthcare professionals to shift from the public to the private sector within Malaysia.[125] To address the acute shortage of healthcare workers, Malaysia's government has introduced a telehealth initiative, which promotes teleconsulting, electronic health records, and online education for healthcare providers. The goals of this program are to upgrade rural access to healthcare, increase the efficiency of current healthcare workers, attract foreign investment to the Multimedia Super Corridor, and encourage clinicians practicing abroad to return home.[126] Additionally, as a more immediate solution, the government has recruited both Malaysian and foreign medical personnel on short-term contracts to serve in the public sector.[127] In 2005, over

50 percent of doctors registered in Malaysia were Chinese or Indian; only 37 percent identified themselves as bumiputra, or ethnic Malay.[128]

Trade and Investment

Malaysia's healthcare industry is served by many domestic and foreign-invested healthcare operations. One leading domestic operation is Kumpulan Perubatan (Johor) Sdn Bhd (KPJSB), the healthcare division of Johor Corporation, a multinational Malaysian corporation. The KPJSB hospital network includes 19 hospitals in Malaysia and 3 in Indonesia, in addition to facilities offering related services such as pathology, pharmaceutical procurement, and hospital management, as well as a nursing college and training programs in clinical and healthcare management.[129] KPJSB also owns KPJ

Healthcare, which was Malaysia's first local private healthcare establishment.[130] Additionally, many foreign firms have entered the Malaysian healthcare market, primarily through joint ventures. Consistent with foreign investment in other areas of Southeast Asia, foreign-owned healthcare facilities in Malaysia have been established primarily in urban areas, catering to middle- and upper-income patients.[131] For example, Columbia Asia Sdn Bhd, a joint venture between the Malay government-run Employees Provident Fund (30 percent) and the U.S.-based Columbia Pacific Healthcare Sdn Bhd (70 percent), has opened six hospitals in Malaysia and plans to open five more.[132] Singaporean hospital system Parkway Holdings Ltd. owns majority shares in two Malaysian hospitals (Gleneagles Medical Centre, Penang and Gleneagles Intan Medical Centre, Kuala Lumpur) and is the operating partner and minority shareholder in Pantai Holdings Bhd, which operates eight Pantai hospitals throughout the country.[133]

Malaysia maintains a number of restrictions on foreign participation in the healthcare sector. Foreign investment is limited to 30 percent, although higher levels of ownership may be permitted with approval from the Ministry of Health.[134] As of 2001, foreign entry into the market was limited to hospitals with at least 100 beds.[135] Additional requirements reported in 2001 appeared to be driven by labor market considerations. Employment of foreign nurses was limited to the private sector; employment of foreign specialists was limited to two per hospital, and such specialists could only treat Malaysian patients; and employment of foreign nurses and specialists was subject to an economic needs test. It is not clear if these barriers have since been liberalized.

Public and private efforts have spawned a profitable medical tourism industry in Malaysia. The number of foreign patients visiting Malaysia for medical treatment increased from 174,189 in 2004 to 374,063 in 2008, generating RM299.1 million ($82.3 million) in revenue in 2008.[136] Within the ASEAN region, Malaysia is the third largest exporter of healthcare services, following Thailand and Singapore.[137]

Malaysia's healthcare facilities attract foreign patients from rich and poor countries alike. Efforts to promote medical tourism targeted less-developed countries, such as Indonesia and Bangladesh, where specialized services are not readily available.[138] However, Malaysia's low costs also make it competitive with Thailand, a traditional medical tourism destination for visitors from developed countries.[139] The private healthcare industry has supported the development of medical tourism by developing a list of recommended fees for common services sought by foreign patients.[140] The publication of such fees increases transparency and is an attempt to the standardize prices charged by providers. The government also provides strong support, as it sees medical tourism as an important component of Malaysia's evolution from a manufacturing to a service economy. In addition to promoting 35 of the country's hospitals as medical tourism providers, the government offers tax incentives within designated "wellness zones" for companies providing services to foreign citizens.[141]

The government has encouraged private healthcare institutions to acquire accreditation or certification in order to promote medical tourism. As a result, most medical centers have either received government accreditation from the Malaysian Society for the Quality of Health or international accreditation via MS ISO 9002.[142] Accreditation by universally recognized, industry-specific organizations provides quality assurance, particularly for Western visitors, and is critical to Malaysia's ability to attract foreign patients in the competitive Southeast Asian market. Penang Adventist Hospital became the first Malaysian hospital to achieve such status when it received Joint Commission International (JCI) accreditation in 2007.[143] There are now five JCI-accredited hospitals in Malaysia (including Penang Adventist) and one accredited ambulatory care center.[144]

Another factor strengthening Malaysia's international competitiveness as a provider of healthcare services is its status as a Muslim country.[145] Middle Eastern countries have been identified as a key market for Malaysia's medical tourism services, a trend which began following September 11, 2001, as Muslim travelers became reluctant to visit Western countries due to political and visa difficulties.[146] Malaysian healthcare providers and marketers emphasize the availability of halal food and other conveniences for practicing Muslims, and this type of marketing is likely the reason Pantai Holdings reports a growing volume of patients from other Islamic countries, such as Indonesia.[147] The Malaysian private healthcare market also has benefited from the creation of a Muslim-specific financial instrument, an Islamic real estate investment trust (REIT). The Islamic healthcare REIT provides Muslim investors with a Sharia-compliant international investment opportunity while also generating financial support for Malaysian healthcare facilities. For example, KPJ Healthcare sponsors Al-'Aqar KPJ REIT, which purchased five KPJ hospitals for RM170 million (US $50 million) and became the first listed Islamic REIT in 2006.[148]

Some Malaysian healthcare firms invest internationally, providing services in foreign markets through joint venture arrangements. For example, a subsidiary of Pantai Holdings has entered into a joint venture with a Saudi Arabian firm to provide healthcare services and open two hospitals in Saudi Arabia.[149] Additionally, the company has voiced intentions to expand into West Asia, India, and Sri Lanka.[150]

Malaysia's Commitments on Healthcare Services under the GATS

With respect to healthcare services, Malaysia's 2005 GATS offer is nearly identical to its 1994 schedule of commitments. Malaysia's offer includes commitments on private hospital services only and, as previously noted, requires that foreign hospital service providers meet an economic needs test and set themselves up as a locally incorporated joint venture with a Malaysian entity. However, Malaysia's offer raises the ceiling for foreign equity in such a joint venture to 40 percent from the 30 percent noted in its 1994 schedule.[151] The Malaysian government has designated healthcare as one of several strategic service sectors to promote economic growth; in 2009, it reportedly lifted foreign investment restrictions on select healthcare services.[152]

Logistics

Overview

Malaysia's core logistics sector includes firms offering cargo handling, storage and warehousing, and freight forwarding, while related subsectors provide road, rail, maritime, air freight transport, and courier services. In 2005, Malaysia had 226 cargo handling establishments employing 7,025 full-time workers, with an output of $282 million; 36 storage and warehousing establishments employing 17,272 full-time workers, with an output of $150 million; and 976 freight forwarding establishments employing 14,998 full-time workers with an output of $1.1 billion. Each of these subsectors demonstrated strong growth in recent years: between 2004 and 2005, the number of establishments, total output, and full-time employees in the cargo handling segment almost doubled, while the output of freight forwarding establishments increased by 51 percent. Storage and warehousing firms have steadily increased their output by an average of 64 percent per year since 2000. Domestic suppliers dominate this market segment, as 98 percent of cargo handling establishments, 97 percent of freight forwarding firms, and all storage and warehousing firms were owned by Malaysian residents in 2005.[153]

Malaysia's recent economic growth has prompted the development of an efficient logistics sector capable of transporting manufactured products to international markets quickly and inexpensively.[154] The sector's health, however, has strengthened and weakened with the country's export volumes.[155] The importance of exports to the logistics sector is illustrated by the fact that, of a total of $12.5 billion invested in 1,007 logistics projects in 2006, $9.8 billion (78 percent) went towards 429 export-oriented projects.[156]

The regional context is an important element in the sector's prospects for expansion. As a result of overall economic growth (and growth in Chinese exports specifically), improved political openness, and increasing trade and investment flows in Southeast Asia, the region's logistics industry is expected to grow significantly through 2017.[157] Malaysian ports and logistics firms compete and measure themselves against their Singaporean counterparts, as Singapore is the established logistics hub in the region. Logistics managers for manufacturing firms consider factors such as transport costs and infrastructure when deciding where to establish plants. In general, firms interested in minimizing costs and accessing stable, high-volume markets set up facilities in Malaysia, while firms that place more value on workforce quality, overall infrastructure, business services, and supportive government policies locate in Singapore.[158]

Malaysia is emerging as a logistics hub for halal food products, and is positioned to capture much of the global halal logistics market, worth an estimated $28 billion to $57 billion in 2005.[159] The halal designation requires dedicated "cold chain"-like protocols throughout the supply chain to ensure compliance with Islamic teachings.[160] Malaysian-based MISC Integrated

Logistics has developed a halal certification process for cargo processing and is investing in a 41-acre halal storage and processing system in Port Klang's free trade zone. Malaysia's government is also planning to construct an industrial food park for halal products.

Government Policies and Sector Reform

In recent years, the Malaysian logistics industry has benefited from government efforts to improve the sector's efficiency by developing and implementing market-friendly policies. Among these are the Integrated Logistics Services (ILS) incentives established in 2002, which encourage integration and consolidation among specialized service logistics providers.[161] As of December 2007, 20 companies have taken advantage of ILS incentives, investing $1.2 billion in logistics consolidation.[162] Malaysia's government has also made substantial investments in roads, resulting in well-maintained highways that support efficient overland shipping, and is participating in a proposed 5,500-kilometer trans-Asia railway linking Singapore, Malaysia, Thailand, Cambodia, Burma, Laos, Vietnam, and China.

The Malaysian Ministry of International Trade and Industry's Third Industrial Master Plan, initiated in 2006, sets out ambitious goals for the country's logistics sector. Its targets for the industry for 2020 include 8.6 percent growth, with the industry ultimately generating 12.1 percent of GDP; growth in total marine cargo to 751 million tons (from 253 million tons in 2005); growth in total air cargo trade to 2.4 million tons (from 1 million tons in 2005); and growth in rail freight volume to 18.6 million tons (from 4 million tons in 2005).[163] Malaysia intends to accomplish these goals by integrating its logistics industry with broader industrialization efforts and with global supply chains. It is also investing in new information and communication technologies, and has made efforts to strengthen inter-ministry and -agency policy coordination.

Trade and Investment

A large number of third-party logistics (3PL) providers—such as Tiong Nam, Linfox, and Trans-Asia Shipping Corp, among others—supply services to Malaysian firms. In one survey, conducted in 2000, 68 percent of all Malaysian firms contracted with 3PL firms instead of conducting logistics in-house (similar to the 65 percent rate for firms in the United States and the 60 percent rate for firms in Singapore).[164] Malaysian firms use 3PL providers extensively for international shipping, with 66 percent of the survey's respondents contracting with 3PL firms to manage both domestic and international logistics. The services most often outsourced were fleet management, shipment consolidation, freight payment, carrier selection, and warehouse management.

In 2007, seaborne shipping accounted for 95 percent (by volume) of Malaysia's total trade in goods.[165] The country's main ports are Port Klang (the 17th busiest port in the world) and Port Tanjung Pelepas, known as PTP (the 19th busiest port). These ports are advantageously located on the Straights of Malacca, the shortest shipping lane between Singapore and the Suez Canal (figure 6).[166] Port Klang, which is served by two port operating companies (Westports and Northport), handled 7.2 million 20-foot equivalent units (TEUs)[167] in 2007, compared to 6.3 million the previous year.[168] PTP, regulated by the Johor Port Authority, handled 5.4 million TEUs in 2007,[169] shortly after the rapid expansion of its shipping services and container volume capacity to a maximum of 8 million TEUs annually.[170] (These impressive gains are still dwarfed by traffic at the busiest port in the world, Singapore, which handled 27.9 million TEUs in 2007.)[171] Malaysia's 33 ports posted record processing numbers in 2007 as a result of increased transshipment traffic (which accounts for 50 percent of Malaysia's total seaborne container trade).[172] The U.S. Container Security Act, implemented in 2004, provides for stringent checks by U.S. representatives on exports at these ports.[173]

Kuala Lumpur International Airport (KLIA)—which is located 50 km from the capital city and is connected to all parts of Malaysia by well-maintained highways—is the hub of air-based logistics, handling 700,000 TEUs in 2005.

Its regional competitors are the Hong Kong International Airport (which handled 2 million TEUs in 2005), Singapore's Changi International Airport (1 million TEUs in 2005), and Bangkok's new Suvarnabhumi Airport (the old airport in Bangkok handled 900,000 TEUs in 2005).[174] KLIA recently offered a three-year waiver of landing fees to increase its market share in regional passenger and freight transport.[175]

All foreign air cargo shipments entering the country at KLIA are handled by MASkargo, the state-owned air cargo carrier, which usually clears goods within 20 minutes of their arrival.[176] MASkargo has made significant improvements in its operations since 2000: establishing written performance standards, providing online tracking and payment processing, and initiating a

Priority Business Center offering premium shipping services to major customers.[177] In 2006, MASkargo generated approximately 18 percent of Malaysian Airlines' total revenue, and despite rising oil prices, MASkargo has been consistently profitable even in years when its parent airline has lost money.[178] MASkargo is also responsible for customs clearance, and thus most air cargo entering or leaving the country passes through MASkargo's 108-acre Advanced Cargo Center at LIA. [179] The Advanced Cargo Center has tight security, which was recently improved due to concerns about bird flu and severe acute respiratory syndrome (SARS).[180]

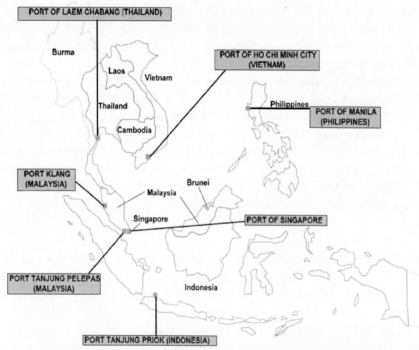

Sourse: Created by commission staff using port ionformation from World Ports Source. http://www.worldportsource.com/ports/region.10.php (accessed April 20, 2009).

Figure 6. Major shipping ports of Southeast Asia.

Overland logistics in Malaysia are also handled primarily by MASkargo Logistics Sdn Bhd, formerly known as Pengangkutan Kargo Udara MAS (PKUM), a subsidiary of MASkargo and the largest trucking company in the country. PKUM has a fleet of 20 trucks (with capacities of 8 to 20 tons) designed to transport pallets and containers, as well as 20,000 square feet of dedicated warehouse space at KLIA.[181]

MASkargo also sells freight and logistics services to customers worldwide through a network of general sales agents, competing with major multinational airlines like Asiana Airlines, Singapore Airlines, Korean Airlines, and Polar Air in providing freight transportation services to Malaysian customers. Malaysia relies heavily on imports of freight services for transportation of its goods, especially during periods of strong activity in Malaysia's merchandise export sectors. During these periods, much of the high demand for logistics services is met by foreign providers (including express operators like DHL, FedEx, UPS, and TNT, along with 3PL providers like Kuehne and Nagel, Exel, Maersk, and Tibbett and Britten, among others).[182] These firms have expanded their operations in Southeast Asia to take advantage of regional growth in the logistics market.

Malaysia's exports of transportation services decreased as a percentage of total commercial services, from 22 percent in 1995 to 19 percent in 2004, partly as a result of competitive pressure from Singaporean logistics firms which have become regional leaders.[183] However, discrete data on Malaysian trade in logistics services are not provided in Ministry of Finance economic reports, but Malaysia exported an estimated $5.8 billion and imported about $11.3 billion in transportation services in 2007, yielding a $5.5 billion balance of payments deficit in this industry segment.[184]

Malaysia's Commitments on Logistics Services under the GATS

Malaysia's 2005 GATS offer includes limited commitments on maritime transport services, but no commitments on distribution services, or on air, road, or rail transportation services. For maritime services, commitments pertain to international maritime transportation services, maritime agency services (which were not included in Malaysia's 1994 GATS schedule), and vessel salvage and refloating services. However, Malaysia's offer on maritime services restricts the forms of commercial establishment available to foreign firms, specifying that commercial presence must occur through a representative office, a regional office, or a joint-venture corporation. Moreover, for international maritime transport services and maritime agency services, foreign equity participation in joint ventures with Malaysian firms is limited to 30 percent. For vessel salvage and refloating services, joint ventures must include bumiputra shareholding of at least 30 percent.[185] Malaysia's most recent trade policy review under the WTO indicates that the Malaysian government eliminated foreign equity restrictions in certain subsectors of transportation services in 2009, but that government-linked companies continue to play an important role in this sector.[186]

Outside of the GATS, Malaysia has taken steps towards improving market access for some foreign providers of logistics services. In 2004, Malaysia and Hong Kong negotiated an "open capacity" air services agreement, which granted their respective airlines "fifth freedom" rights (i.e., permission to carry passengers and cargo between the two countries and onto third countries).[187] ASEAN members have agreed to allow investors from other ASEAN countries to acquire equity holdings in logistics firms of as much as 49 percent by the end of 2008, 51 percent by 2010, and 70 percent by 2013.[188] Currently, Malaysia allows equity holdings by non-ASEAN foreigners of up to 70 percent in shipping companies and 49 percent in freight forwarding agencies, with non-foreign equity being specifically allocated to bumiputras.[189]

TOPICS FOR FURTHER ANALYSIS

Research and analysis presented in this paper indicate that the Malaysian government has used various measures to promote the development of its service industries. Policies pursued by the government of Malaysia in the three sectors analyzed—including promoting consolidation within the banking sector, encouraging the development of private hospitals, and investing in port facilities—seek to strengthen the industries and ultimately increase exports. The Malaysian government has liberalized some barriers to the foreign provision of services, and recent liberalization could result in an increase in services exports to that country.

There are several aspects of the Malaysian service sector that may merit further investigation. Future research might examine additional Malaysian service industries, particularly the passenger air services and insurance industries. Passenger air services are a significant and growing component of Malaysian service exports, accounting for about 9 percent of such exports in 2006 following an average annual increase of 19 percent from 2002 through 2006. Analysis of the insurance industry would provide an example of a Malaysian industry in which foreign suppliers have a significant presence.[190]

Further comparisons of Malaysia's service sector with the service sectors of other nations would underscore the significance of services to the Malaysian economy and provide context for Malaysia's overall position in global services trade. Finally, additional research examining the effect of previous service liberalization on the Malaysian economy could lead to the refinement of econometric methods of predicting the potential effect of further liberalization on Malaysian services trade.

APPENDIX

Table A.1. Summary statistics 2000–06

Variable	Obser vations	Mean	Standard Deviation	Minimum	Maximum
ln (services imports)	4582	4.54	2.53	-4.91	10.66
ln (importer's GDP)	4554	25.92	1.47	22.45	29.26
ln (exporter's GDP)	4682	26.34	1.36	23.73	30.05
ln (distance)	4682	8.15	1.12	4.09	9.87
ln (importer's remoteness)	4682	-12.60	0.91	-13.86	-10.98
ln (exporter's remoteness)	4682	-12.07	1.38	-15.99	-9.77
Adjacency	4682	0.07	0.25	0	1
Common language	4682	0.08	0.27	0	1
Services FDI restrictiveness	4682	0.24	0.14	0.04	0.67

Table A.2. Summary statistics 2004

Variable	Obser vations	Mean	Standard Deviation	Minimum	Maximum
ln (services imports)	881	4.72	2.43	-4.39	10.49
ln (importer's GDP)	873	25.92	1.45	22.74	29.22
ln (exporter's GDP)	897	26.28	1.31	23.87	29.99
ln (distance)	897	8.13	1.12	4.09	9.87
ln (importer's remoteness)	897	-14.29	0.92	-15.56	-12.56
ln (exporter's remoteness)	897	-12.33	0.59	-20.11	-11.83
Adjacency	897	0.07	0.25	0	1
Common language	897	0.08	0.27	0	1
Services FDI restrictiveness	897	0.24	0.14	0.04	0.67

Table A.3. Correlation matrix 2000–06

	$\ln Y_i$	$\ln Y_j$	$\ln D_{ij}$	$\ln REM_i$	$\ln REM_j$	A_{ij}	CL_{ij}	$SFDIR_{ij}$
$\ln Y_i$	1.00							
$\ln Y_j$	0.10							
$\ln D_{ij}$	0.20	1.00						
$\ln REM_i$	0.29	0.14	1.00					
$\ln REM_j$	-0.12	0.07	0.79	1.00				
A_{ij}	0.07	-0.97	-0.09	-0.07	1.00			
CL_{ij}	0.05	0.03	-0.44	-0.19	-0.06	1.00		
$SFDIR_{ij}$	0.05	0.10	0.04	0.10	-0.07	0.18	1.00	
		0.03	0.44	0.56	-0.02	-0.11	0.06	1.00

Table A.4. Correlation matrix 2004

	$\ln Y_i$	nY_j	$\ln D_{ij}$	$\ln REM_i$	$\ln REM_j$	A_{ij}	CL_{ij}	$SFDIR_{ij}$
$\ln Yi$	1.00							
$\ln Yj$	0.09							
$\ln Dij$	0.21	1.00						
$\ln REMi$	0.26	0.14	1.00					
$\ln REMj$	-0.18	0.06 -	0.81	1.00				
Aij	0.06	0.39	-0.06	-0.06	1.00			
$CLij$	0.06	0.03	-0.44	-0.21	-0.10	1.00		
$SFDIRij$	0.07	0.09	0.03	0.09	-0.06	0.19	1.00	
		0.04	0.46	0.56	-0.02	-0.12	0.06	1.00

BIBLIOGRAPHY

Ahmad, Natila. *Healthcare Sector Overview*. U.S. Department of Commerce. U.S. Commercial Service, September 26, 2001.

Airline Business. "Asian Cargo Opens Up," vol. 20, no. 4 (April 2004): 25.

Ali, Sharidan. "Dubai-Based Operator Pulls Out of PKFZ." *The Star Online*, July 19, 2007. http://biz.thestar.com.my/news/story.asp?file=/2007/7/19 /business/18344875&sec.

American Association of Port Authorities. "World Port Ratings: 2007," n.d.http://www.aapaports.org/Industry/content.cfm?ItemNumber =900&navItemNumber=551 (accessed June 12, 2009).

Arunanondchai, Jutamas, and Carsten Fink. *Trade in Health Services in the ASEAN Region*. World Bank. World Bank Policy Research Working Paper 4147, March 2007. http://www-wds.worldbank.org/external/default

/WDSContentServer/IW3P/IB/2007/02/22/000016406200702221010411/R endered /PDF/ wps4147.pdf.

Bank Negara Malaysia. "The Financial Sector Masterplan," 2001. http://www.bnm.gov.my/index.php?ch=20.

———. "Commercial Banks: Statement of Assets of Domestic and Foreign Banks," n.d. (accessed May 10, 2010).

———. "Islamic Banking System, Statement of Assets (as of 31 March 2010)." *Monthly Statistical Bulletin*, March 14, 2010. http://www.bnm.gov.my/files/publication/msb/2008/4/pdf/2.31.pdf.

———. "List of Banking Institutions (as of 31 May 2008)." *Monthly Statistical Bulletin*, May 31, 2008. http://www.bnm.gov.my/files/publication/msb/2008/5/pdf/2.3.pdf.

Bhatnagar, Rohit, Jayanth Jayaram, and Yue Cheng Phua. "Relative Importance of Plant Location Factors: A Cross National Comparison Between Singapore and Malaysia." *Journal of Business Logistics* 24, no. 1 (March 2003): 147–70.

Bumiputra-Commerce Holdings Berhad. *Annual Report 2007*, 2007. http://www.cimb.com/annual_reports/BCHB/2007/index.html.

———. *Annual Report 2008*, 2008, 149.

Business Development Asia. "Malaysia." *Asian Health Newsletter*, no. 51 (June 2007): 6.

Business Monitor International. "Key Sectors." *Malaysia Business Forecast Report* 4th Quarter, 2006: 36–46. http://search.ebscohost.com /login.aspx?direct=true&db=buh&AN=21975129&site=ehost -live.

Cheen, Lim Chze. "Malaysia: Strategies for the Liberalization of the Services Sector." *WTO: Managing the Challenges of WTO Participation*; *Case Study 25*, n.d. http://www.wto.org/english/res e/booksp e/casestudies e/case25 e.htm.

Columbia Asia. "Columbia Asia Plans Aggressive Expansion in Malaysia." News release, April 21, 2009.

Danish Trade Council. *The Health Care Sector*. Royal Danish Embassy, Kuala Lumpur, Malaysia. January 6, 2005. http://www.ambkualalumpur. um.dk/NR/rdonlyres/591284AC-AB7E-4376-9A22-00145E297993/0/ TheHealthCareSector.pdf.

———. Royal Danish Embassy, Kuala Lumpur Malaysia. *The Health Care Sector*, March 31, 2009.

Department of Statistics Malaysia. Economic Census 2006 Malaysia: Health. December 2007.

———. Economic Census 2004 Malaysia: Health. December 2005.

————. *Economic Census 2006 Malaysia: Transport and Communications*, December 2007.

————. "Health Services (Private Sector)," November 3, 2009.

————. "Number and Percentage of Registered Professionals by Ethnic Group, 2006." Yearbook of Statistics Malaysia, 2007, 235, table 9.3.

Dewi, K Kasturi. "Hospitals Set Fees for Health Tourism." The Star, October 28, 2003. http://www.hospitals-malaysia.org/newsmaster.cfm?&menuid =38&parentid=28&action=view&retrieveid=259.

Economist Intelligence Unit (EIU). *Country Commerce: Malaysia*. New York: Economist Intelligence Unit, June 2009.http://www.eiu. com/index.asp? layout=displayIssueArticle&issue_id=1753435360&opt=f ull.

————. *Country Profile 2007: Malaysia*. London: Economist Intelligence Unit, 2007. http://www.eiu.com/report dl.asp?issue id=1612811546 &mode=pdf.

————. *Country Profile 2008: Malaysia*. London: Economist Intelligence Unit, 2008. http://www.eiu.com/report dl.asp?issue id=161285586& mode=pdf.

————. *Country Report: Malaysia*. London: Economist Intelligence Unit, May 2008. http://www.eiu.com/report_dl.asp?issue_id= 613374246& mode=pdf.

————. *Country Report: Malaysia*. London: Economist Intelligence Unit, June 2009.

————. *Country Finance: Malaysia*, 2006, 16.

————. *Country Finance: Malaysia,* 2007, 3, 14.

————. *Country Finance: Malaysia,* 2009, 14.

————. "EIU Data Tool." http://data.eiu.com/default.aps (accessed various dates).

El-Gamal, Mahmoud Amin. *Overview of Islamic Finance*. Office of International Affairs Occasional Paper 4. U.S. Department of Treasury, Office of International Affairs, August 2006. http://www.treas.gov /offices/international-affairs/occasional-paperseries/08042006 OccasionalPaper4.pdf.

Filat-Castejón, Carmen, Joseph F. Francois, and Julia Wörz, "Cross-Border Trade and FDI in Services." February 2009.

Ganesan, Vasantha. "Taking the Sting out of Medical Bills." *New Straits Times*, March 10, 2007.

Golub, Stephen. "Openness to Foreign Direct Investment in Services: An International Comparative Analysis." *World Economy*, vol. 32, issue 8, August 2009, 1245-1268.

Government of Malaysia. Prime Minister's Department. Economic Planning Unit. *Ninth Malaysia Plan*, 2006–2010. Putrajava, 2006.

———.*Tenth Malaysia Plan*, 2011–2015. Putrajaya, 2010.

Grünfeld, Leo A., and Andreas Moxnes. "The Intangible Globalization: Explaining the Patterns of International Trade in Services." Norwegian Institute of International Affairs. Working Paper 657, 2003.

———. "The Intangible Globalization," 2003, 7.

———. "The Intangible Globalization," 2003, 20–21.

Haq, Robeel. "Halal Logistics Hits the Middle East." ITPBusiness.net, May 29, 2006. http://www.halaljournal.com/artman/publish/article_ 793.shtml.

Hashim, Salmy. "Bumi Preferences Pose a Hurdle in U.S.-Malaysia FTA Talks." Bernama.com, January 13, 2007. http://www.bernama.com /bernama/v3/printable.php?id =241114.

Helpman, Elhanan, Marc Melitz, and Yona Rubinstein. "Estimating Trade Flows: Trading Partners and Trading Volumes." NBER Worker Paper W12927, February 2007, 1.

Inland Review Board of Malaysia. "Tax Relief Summary: List of Tax Relief for Resident Individuals 2010," n.d. (accessed January 4, 2010).

International Monetary Fund (IMF). Balance of Payments Manual, 1993. http://imf.org/external/pubs/ft/bopman/bopman.pdf.

———."Balance of Payments and International Investment Position Manual, Sixth Edition (BPM6)," December 2008, 263–266.

———. "Representative Exchange Rates for Selected Currencies for December 2008," n.d. (accessed January 4, 2010).

———. "Representative Exchange Rates for Selected Currencies for January 2010," n.d. (accessed January 4, 2010).

Islamic Finance News. "Al-'Aqar KPJ REIT: The World's First Listed Islamic Healthcare REIT." Deals of the Year 2006 Handbook, n.d. http://www.islamicfinancenews.com/HanbookPDF/8.Al-Aqar.pdf (accessed June 24, 2008).

Islamic Foods and Nutrition Council of America. "Frequently Asked Questions: What Is Halal?" http://www.ifanca.org/halal/ (accessed June 29, 2009).

Japanese Ministry of Economy, Trade and Industry (METI). Report on Compliance by Major Trading Partners with Trade Agreements: WTO, FTA/EPA, BIT, April 2007. http://www meti.go.jp/English/report /data/gCT07_1coe.html (accessed October 8, 2009).

Johor Corporation Web site. "Corporate Profile," n.d. http://www.jcorp. com.my/ (accessed June 24, 2008).

Joint Commission International. "Joint Commission International (JCI) Accredited Organizations," 2007. http://www.jointcommission international.org/23218/iortiz/ (accessed multiple dates).

Khoon, Chan Chee. "Privatizing the Welfare State: Health Care Reforms in Malaysia." *New Solutions* 13, no. 1 (2003): 87–105.

Kimura, Fukunari, and Hyun-Hoon Lee. "The Gravity Equation in International Trade in Services."*Review of World Economics* 142, no. 1 (April 2006): 92 – 121.

Leng, Chee Heng. *Medical Tourism in Malaysia: International Movement of Healthcare Consumers and the Commodification of Healthcare.* Asia Research Institute. National University of Singapore. Asia Research Institute Working Paper Series 83, January 2007. http://www.ari.nus.edu. sg/docs/ wps/wps07 083.pdf.

Mahmood, Amir. "Malaysia's Export Competitiveness in Services and the Third Malaysia Industrial Master Plan: Issues, Assessment, and Prospects," October 8, 2007. http://www.epu.gov.my/mdi1/mdi/ files/ Malaysian Services Trade EPU2007 SV.pdf.

Malaysia Industrial Development Authority. "Services Sector Overview," n.d. http://www.mida.gov.my/en_v2/index.php?page=services-sector (accessed January 10, 2010).

———. "Malaysia's Growing Logistics Services," February 23, 2007.

Malaysian-German Chamber of Commerce and Industry. "Market Watch 2010: The Healthcare Sector in Malaysia," n.d. (accessed January 10, 2010).

Malaysian Industrial Development Authority (MIDA). "Promotion of Services in Malaysia." *Investment Opportunities in the Services Sector*, April 27, 2007. http://www.mida.gov.my/. (accessed January 10, 2010).

Mark, Ken. "Global Ambition: Malaysia." *Canadian Transportation & Logistics* 110, no. 10 (October 2007): 28–31.

MASkargo. "Kargo Udara Mas," n.d. http://www.maskargo.com/module. php?folder=products&filename=pkum (accessed July 2, 2008).

Maybank Group. *Annual Report 2007,* September 7, 2007. http://www.maybank2u.com.my/corporate/financial info.shtml.

———. *Annual Report 2009*, 2009, 58.

Meng, YB Dato' Chua Jui. "The Briefing Session for Contract Doctors from the Arab Republic of Egypt." Transcript of speech, March 2, 2004. http://www.moh.gov.my/MohPortal/speechDetail.jsp?action=view&id=79

Ministry of Health Malaysia. "Bahagian Telekesihatan (Telehealth Flagship Project)," n.d. http://www.moh.gov.my/opencms/ opencms/moh/bhg_ telekesihatan.html (accessed June 19, 2008).

——. *Health Facts 2004*, October 2005. ——. *Health Facts 2008*, May 2009.

Ministry of International Trade and Industry Malaysia. "Industry Profile: Services: Healthcare," n.d. http://www.miti.gov.my/cms/content.jsp? id=com.tms.cms.section.Section_6393a556- c0a8156f-5cff5cff-ecbc 7990 (accessed June 2008).

——. *Malaysia: International Trade and Industry Report 2007*, July 2008. http://www.miti.gov.my.

——. *Malaysia: International Trade and Industry Report 2008*, July 2009. http://www.miti.gov.my.

——. "Official Portal of Ministry of International Trade and Industry Malaysia," n.d. http://www.miti.gov.my/cms/index.jsp (accessed July 2, 2008).

——. Telephone interview by USITC staff, August 8, 2008.

Ministry of Tourism Malaysia. "Tax Incentives," n.d.http://www2.motour. gov.my/index.php/english/tax.html (accessed June 3, 2008).

New Straits Times (Business Times). "Pantai to Expand Overseas Ops," December 7, 2004. http://www.pantai.com.my/site.cfm? hid=7&sec =newslet&prMode=0&pr select=63.

Organisation for Economic Co-operation and Development . OECD. Stat Extracts: Trade in Services by Partner Country Database (accessed August 2009).

ParkwayHealth. "Global Presence," n.d. http://www.parkwayhealth.com/ Management/Global Presence.asp (accessed June 25, 2008).

Portsworld.com Malaysia. "Port Klang Authority," n.d. http://www. portsworld.com/portauthorities/pka.htm (accessed November 2, 2007).

——. "Record Performance by Malaysian Ports," February 11, 2008. http://www.portsworld.com/news/pw1feb11 08.htm.

Public Bank Berhad. *Annual Report 2007*, 2007. http://ww2.publicbank. com.my/. Putzger, Ian. "Grounded." *Journal of Commerce (15307557)* 7, no. 38 (2006): 44–45.

——. "MAS Momentum." *Air Cargo World* 92, no. 6 (June 2002): 18–21.

——. "Searching for Space." *Air Cargo World* 97, no. 3 (March 2007): 32– 38.

Rasiah, Rajah. "Trade-Related Investment Liberalization under the WTO: The Malaysian Experience." *Global Economic Review* 34, no. 4 (December 2005): 453–71. http://www.tandf.co.uk/journals/titles/1226508x.asp.

Shaw, Charles. "Accreditation and ISO: International Convergence on Health Care Standards." *International Journal for the Quality in Health Care* 9, no. 1 (1997): 11–13.

Small and Medium Industries Development Corporation (SMIDC). "SME Annual Report 2008," 2009. http://www.smidec.gov.my/ (accessed May 13, 2010).

———."Definition of SMEs by Size," 2008. http://www/smidec. gov.my /detailpage.jsp?page=defsme (accessed June 29, 2009).

———. "SME Information & Advisory Centre: Statistics," 2008. http://www.smidec.gov.my/detailpage.jsp?statistic (accessed June 29, 2009).

———. "SME Information & Advisory Centre: Financial Assistance Scheme for SMEs in the Services Sectors," 2008. http://www.smidec.gov.my /detailpage.jsp?statistic (accessed July 7, 2009).

Sohail, M. Sadiq, Rohit Bhatnagar, and Amrik S. Sohal. "A Comparative Study on the Use of Third Party Logistics Services by Singaporean and Malaysian Firms." *International Journal of Physical Distribution and Logistics Management* 36, no. 9 (November 2006): 690–701.

Sun, The. "Pantai: Health Tourism to Drive Growth," September 15, 2004. http://www.pantai.com.my/site.cfm?hid=1&sec=newslet&prMode=0&pr select=61.

Tinbergen, Jan. *Shaping the World Economy: Suggestions for an International Economic Policy.* (Twentieth Century Fund: New York), 1962.

Tongzon, Jose. "Determinants of Competitiveness in Logistics: Implications for the ASEAN Region." *Maritime Economics and Logistics* 9, no. 1 (March 2007): 67–83. http://www.palgrave-journals.com/mel/.

Tourism Malaysia. Advertising and Publicity Division. "Health Tourism in Malaysia," November 5, 2007. http://www. tourism. gov.my/ tourismbiz /media_centre/articles/travelideas/PR%20Health% 20Tourism%206%20Nov%2007.pdf.

Treasury Malaysia. *Economic Report 2007/2008*, 2007. http://www.Treasury. gov.my/inoex.php?che33*pg=165+ac=2053+lang=eng.

———. *Economic Report 2008/2009*, 2008. http://www.treasury. gov.my/ ndex.php?option=com_content+view=article_id=776%3Alaporan-elconomi-20082009+calid=73%3Asenarai-laporan-ekaromi+Trend=174* lang=en.

————. *Economic Report 2009/2010*, 2009. http://www.treasury.gov.my /index.php?option=com_content&view=article&id=1340%3 Alaporan-ekonomi-20092010&catid=73%3Asenarai-laporanekonomi& Itemid= 174 &lang=en.

U.N. World Tourism Organization (UNWTO). *Yearbook of Tourism Statistics, 2006 and 2008,*
_____. CDROM.

United States Trade Representative (USTR). "Malaysia." *2008 National Trade Estimate Report on Foreign Trade Barriers*, 2008. http://www.ustr. gov/assets/Document_Library/Reports_Publications/2008/2008_NTE_R eport/asset upload file356 14651.pdf.

U.S. Department of Commerce (USDOC). Bureau of Economic Analysis (BEA). "U.S. International Services: Cross-Border Trade in 2007 and Sales through Affiliates in 2006." *Survey of Current Business* 88, no. 10 (October 2008): 16–62.

————. "U.S. International Services: Cross-Border Trade in 2008 and Sales Through Affiliates in 2007." *Survey of Current Business* 89, no.10 (October 2009): 40–64.

U.S. Department of State. "Background Note: Malaysia," December 2008. http://www.state.gov/r/pa/ei/bgn/2777.htm.

U.S. Foreign and Commercial Service (US&FCS) and U.S. Department of State. *Doing Business in Malaysia: 2008 Country Commercial Guide*, February 21, 2008. http://www.buyusainfo.net/docs/x 8631291.pdf.

Walsh, Keith. "Trade in Services: Does Gravity Hold? A Gravity Model Approach to Estimating Barriers to Services Trade." Business School, Dublin City University. Institute for International Integration Studies Discussion Paper 183, October 2006. http://www.tcd.ie/iiis/documents/ discussion/pdfs/iiisdp183.pdf.

World Bank. "World Development Indicators (WDI) Online Database." http://ddpext.worldbank.org/ext/DDPQQ /member.do? method=get Members&userid=1&queryId=6 (accessed various dates).

World Health Organization (WHO). *Global Health Statistics 2008*. Geneva: WHO Press, 2008. http://www.who.int/whosis/whostat /EN_WHS08_ Table4_HSR.pdf.

————. "Malaysia." *Country Profiles*, March 2010.

World Trade Organization (WTO). General Agreement on Trade in Services (GATS). "Malaysia: Schedule of Specific Commitments." GATS/SC/52, April 15, 1994.

————. "Malaysia: Revised Offer." TN/S/O/MYS/Rev.1, January 31, 2006.

World Trade Organization (WTO). Trade Policy Review Body. "Trade Policy Review Report by the Secretariat Malaysia Revision." WT/TPR/S/156/Rev.1, March 9, 2006.

————. "Trade Policy Review Report by the Secretariat, Malaysia." WT/TPR/S/225, December 14, 2009.

Yon, Rohaizat. "Financing Health Care in Malaysia: Safety Net for the Disadvanged Groups Including Pensioners, Elderly People, the Poor and the Disabled." *NCD Malaysia* 3, no. 2 (2004): 43–46.

Yong, Elaine. "Tapping Into the Healthcare Services Sector in Malaysia." Australia-Malaysia Business Council, April 15, 2003. http://www.ambcwa.org/articles/Article_Health_Care_services.pdf (accessed June 11, 2008).

Yong, H. E. Ong Keng. "Towards a Free Flow of Services in ASEAN." Presented at the opening of the ASEAN Forum on Trade in Services, Hanoi, Vietnam, July 5, 2005. http://www.aseansec.org/17536.htm.

End Notes

[1] The invaluable assistance of Monica Reed, Patricia M. Cooper, Cindy Payne, and Joann Peterson is gratefully acknowledged. Please direct all correspondence to Jennifer Baumert Powell, Office of Industries, U.S. International Trade Commission, 500 E Street, SW, Washington, DC 20436, telephone: 202-205-3450, fax: 202-205-2359, Email: Jennifer.Powell@usitc.gov.

[1] U.S. Department of Commerce (USDOC), Bureau of Economic Analysis (BEA), "U.S. International Services: Cross-Border Trade in 2008," October 2009, 48–59.

[2] Ibid. The service sector's value-added reported at constant prices as a percentage of nominal GDP at factor cost. GDP at factor cost is GDP at market prices, less indirect taxes, plus subsidies.

[3] Treasury Malaysia, *Economic Report 2009/2010*, 2009.

[4] Ministry of International Trade and Industry Malaysia, *Malaysia: International Trade and Industry Report 2007*, July 2008, 129. These targets for growth are set out in Malaysia's Third Industrial Master Plan and are coordinated by two councils, the Malaysian Services Development Council and the Malaysia Logistics Council.

[5] Economist Intelligence Unit (EIU), *Country Profile 2007: Malaysia*, 2007, 12. Membership in ASEAN is central to Malaysia's foreign policy. Additionally, China and ASEAN are currently negotiating the final part of a free trade agreement, which includes an agreement on services, signed in January 2007. In addition to Malaysia, the members of ASEAN include Brunei Darussalam, Cambodia, Indonesia, Laos, Myanmar, the Philippines, Singapore, Thailand and Vietnam.

[6] U.S. Department of State, "Background Note: Malaysia," December 2008. The United States is Malaysia's largest trading partner.

[7] USDOC, The United States Foreign & Commercial Service (USF&CS), and U.S. Department of State, *Doing Business in Malaysia: 2008 Country Commercial Guide*, February 21, 2008, 2.

[8] Ibid., 3. In May 2004, the U.S. and Malaysia signed a trade and investment framework agreement (TIFA), and in June 2006, bilateral negotiations began on a U.S.-Malaysia Free Trade Agreement (FTA). Eight rounds of negotiations were conducted through June 2008.

[9] The first study in the series is USITC, *An Overview and Examination of the Indian Services Sector*, July 2010, http://www.usitc.gov.

[10] EIU, *Country Profile 2007: Malaysia*, 2007, 31; Treasury Malaysia, *Economic Report 2009/2010*. The Malaysian service sector is divided into intermediate, final, and government services. Intermediate services include transport and storage; communication; finance and insurance; and real estate and business services. Final services consist of utilities; wholesale and retail trade; hotels and restaurants; and other services, which comprise community, social, and personal services, as well as imputed rent of owner-occupied dwellings. Government services are recorded separately.

[11] Treasury Malaysia, *Economic Report 2008/2009*, 2008,Table 3.1; Treasury Malaysia, *Economic Report 2009/2010*, 2009. Malaysian total GDP is reported as sectoral GDP for the agriculture, mining, manufacturing, construction, and services sectors of the Malaysian economy, less undistributed financial intermediate services indirectly measured (FISIM), plus import duties.

[12] World Bank, "World Development Indicators (WDI) Online Database," (various dates). Data on services value added for the world are given in constant 2000 dollars, and are only available through 2005. Growth in other regional countries' services markets is expressed by percentage increase in services value added in 2008.

[13] Treasury Malaysia, *Economic Report 2009/2010*, 2009.

[14] Treasury Malaysia, *Economic Report 2008/2009*, 2008, Table 6.1, and Treasury Malaysia, *Economic Report 2009/2010*, 2009, Table 2.2.

[15] Government services— services consumed by the Malaysian government—accounted for 13.4 percent of Malaysian GDP during that same year. Treasury Malaysia does not define "government services"; however, it is indicated that growth in this sector reflects increased public services spending. Treasury Malaysia, *Economic Report 2009/2010*, 2009.

[16] Treasury Malaysia, *Economic Report 2009/2010*, Table 2.3, 2008.

[17] EIU, *Country Profile 2008: Malaysia*, 2008, 24.

[18] In April 2009, the Malaysian government abolished the rule that bumiputras must own no less than 30 percent of equity in 27 service industries.

[19] SMEs in most Malaysian service sectors either have no more than 50 full-time employees or have annual sales turnover of no more than 5 million ringgits ($1.6 million). However, SMEs in manufacturing-related services, manufacturing, and agricultural based industries have either less than 150 full-time employees or less than 25 million ringgits ($8 million) in annual sales turnover. (1 ringgit = 0.3224 U.S. dollars on September 20, 2010). Small- and Medium-Industries Development Corporation, "Definition of SMEs by Size," 2008.

[20] Small- and Medium-Industries Development Corporation, "SME Annual Report," 2008, 54.

[21] EIU, *Country Profile 2007: Malaysia*, 2007, 30.

[22] Small- and Medium-Industries Development Corporation, "SME Information & Advisory Centre," 2008.

[23] Small- and Medium-Industries Development Corporation, "SME Annual Report," 2008, 37.

[24] Ibid., 31.

[25] EIU, *Country Profile 2007: Malaysia*, 2007, 22, and Economic Planning Unit, Prime Minister's Department, *Ninth Malaysia Plan*, 2006. The Ninth Malaysia Plan is the Malaysian government's current five-year economic plan, which extends until the end of 2010.

[26] Ibid., 18.

[27] Malaysian Industrial Development Authority (MIDA), "Promotion of Services in Malaysia," n.d.

[28] U.N. World Tourism Organization (UNWTO), *Yearbook of Tourism Statistics*, 2006 and 2008. Brunei registered the fastest average annual growth in tourist arrivals to Malaysia (32 percent) from 2002 through 2006, followed by the South Korea (31 percent), the Philippines (18 percent), Thailand (13 percent), Indonesia (12 percent), and India (11 percent). By comparison, from 2002 through 2006, the average annual growth of overall tourist arrivals to Malaysia was 7 percent. The only other countries achieving above-average annual growth in tourist arrivals to Malaysia were Australia and the United States, registering 9 percent and 8 percent growth, respectively.

[29] EIU, "EIU Data Tool" (accessed July 7, 2009). During 2002–06, personal disposable income in the South Korea rose 18.8 percent, and in Indonesia and India, 13.6 percent each. At the same time, in the Philippines, personal disposable income rose an estimated 6.1 percent, and in Thailand, an estimated 4.2 percent.

[30] Malaysian Industrial Development Authority (MIDA), "Promotion of Services in Malaysia," n.d.. These incentive schemes apply to services such as business support services for international procurement centers, regional distribution centers, and operational headquarters; research and development (R&D) services; industrial training, including technical and vocational training; and environmental management services.

[31] Target industries, as identified by MIDA, are real estate, transport, energy, telecommunications, distributive trade, hotel and tourism, financial services, and health services. Malaysian Industrial Development Authority (MIDA),"Services Sector Overview." n.d.

[32] Ministry of International Trade and Industry Malaysia, *Malaysia: International Trade and Industry Report 2008*, 47.

[33] Value converted from ringgits to dollars by USITC staff using the December 31, 2008, interbank rate of RM1 =US$ 0.3336.

[34] Halal and haram—words that respectively mean "permitted" and "prohibited" in Arabic—are used to refer to all aspects of Islamic life. Halal foods include all foods that are not haram, such as pork, animals slaughtered in a certain manner, blood and its by-products, alcohol, and items that have been contaminated by haram products, among others. Islamic Foods and Nutrition Council of America, "Frequently Asked Questions: What Is Halal?" n.d..

[35] EIU, *Country Profile 2007: Malaysia*, 2007, 24.

[36] Treasury Malaysia, *Economic Report 2007/2008*, 2007, Table 3.22.

[37] Ministry of International Trade and Industry Malaysia, telephone interview by USITC staff, August 8, 2008.

[38] EIU, *Country Report: Malaysia*, May 2008, 4; USF&CS and U.S. Department of State, *Doing Business in Malaysia: 2008 Country Commercial Guide*, February 21, 2008, 3.

[39] Ministry of International Trade and Industry Malaysia, telephone interview by USITC staff, August 8, 2008.

[40] USF&CS and U.S. Department of State, *Doing Business in Malaysia: 2008 Country Commercial Guide*, February 21, 2008, 50.

[41] USF&CS and U.S. Department of State, *Doing Business in Malaysia: 2008 Country Commercial Guide*, February 21, 2008, 2–3; Hashim, "Bumi Preferences Pose a Hurdle in U.S.-Malaysia FTA Talks," January 13, 2007.

[42] Ministry of International Trade and Industry Malaysia, telephone interview by USITC staff, August 8, 2008.

[43] Department of Statistics Malaysia, "Number and Percentage of Registered Professionals by Ethnic Group, 2006."

[44] EIU, *Country Commerce: Malaysia,* June 2009.

[45] EIU, *Country Report: Malaysia*, June 2009.

[46] The IMF defines "travel" to include goods and services purchased in a certain market by travelers that are visiting that market for a period of not more than one year. "Travel" does not however include the international transport of passengers, which is captured in IMF statistics on passenger transport. IMF, *Balance of Payments Manual*, 1993, 64.

[47] Other business services include research and development (R&D) services, legal services, accounting, management consulting, public relations services, advertising, market research, public opinion polling, architecture, engineering, environmental remediation, agricultural, mining, leasing, and trade-related services. IMF, "Balance of Payments and International Investment Position Manual, Sixth Edition (BPM6)," December 2008, 263—66.

[48] Malaysia does not report any exports of passenger transport services other than those provided by air transport.

[49] Ibid.

[50] Ibid.

[51] USDOC, BEA, "U.S. International Services: Cross-Border Trade in 2008," October 2009, 48–59.

[52] Data on affiliate transactions lag those on cross-border services trade by one year. Analyses of cross-border trade data compare performance in 2008 to trends from 2003 through 2007. Similarly, analyses of affiliate sales compare performance in 2007, the most recent year for which affiliate sales data are available, to trends from 2004 through 2006. In 2008, BEA changed the method of reporting affiliate trade data. New affiliate data report "services supplied," which better reflect services output than the prior measure "sales of services." Data for years prior to 2004 do not reflect this change, but report sales of services. For more information, see USDOC, BEA, *Survey of Current Business* 89, no. 10, 34–36.

[53] Data are suppressed for years prior to 2006.

[54] The GATS identifies four modes of supply through which services are traded. Mode 1 refers to cross-border trade, in which a service is supplied by an individual or firm in one country to an individual or firm in another country. Mode 2 refers to consumption abroad, in which an individual from one country travels to another country and consumes a service in that country. Mode 3 refers to commercial presence, in which a firm based in one country establishes an affiliate, branch or subsidiary in another country and supplies services from that locally established affiliate, branch or subsidiary. Mode 4 refers to the temporary presence of natural persons, in which an individual service supplier from one country travels to another country on a short-term basis to supply a service there.

[55] WTO, "Trade Policy Review Report by the Secretariat, Malaysia," December 14, 2009, 56.

[56] Cheen, "Malaysia: Strategies for the Liberalization of the Services Sector,", n.d; and WTO, "Trade Policy Review Report by the Secretariat: Malaysia," December 14, 2009, 57.

[57] Yong, "Towards a Free Flow of Services in ASEAN," July 5, 2005.

[58] WTO, "Trade Policy Review Report by the Secretariat: Malaysia Revision," March 9, 2006, 26.

[59] Rasiah, "Trade-Related Investment Liberalization under the WTO," December 2005, 453–71.

[60] Helpman, Melitz, and Rubinstein, "Estimating Trade Flows," February 2007, 1.

[61] Tinbergen, "Shaping the World Economy," 1962.

[62] Grünfeld and Moxnes, "The Intangible Globalization," 2003.

[63] Kimura and Lee, "The Gravity Equation in International Trade in Services," April 2006.

[64] Grünfeld and Moxnes, "The Intangible Globalization," 2003, 7.

[65] Some models use only the share of GDP accounted for by the sector being studied. We ran an alternative model using the service sector's share of GDP instead of overall GDP, and found similar results, but with a smaller effect on the variable that measures restrictiveness on foreign direct investment (FDI) in the services sector (SFDIR). We use overall GDP to reflect the fact that traded services are often intermediate inputs in the production of goods as well as services.

[66] Kimura and Lee, "The Gravity Equation in International Trade in Services," 2006, 95.

[67] Walsh, "Trade in Services," October 2006.

[68] Grünfeld and Moxnes use Trade Restrictiveness Indexes (TRIs) for six service industries developed by the Australian Productivity Commission (APC). Kimura and Lee use the Economic Freedom of the World Index developed by the Fraser Institute. Walsh uses the Heritage Foundation's Index of Economic Freedom, measures of government effectiveness developed by Kaufman et al. of the World Bank, the APC TRIs, and measures based on GATS commitments developed by Hoekman (1995). Walsh runs sector-specific regressions as well as ones for all services trade.

[69] Golub, "Openness to Foreign Direct Investment in Services," 2009.

[70] The literature examining the relationship between FDI and cross-border trade is more extensive for trade in goods than for trade in services. Some of these studies point to substitutive effects as well. See, for example, Blonigen, "In Search of Substitution between Foreign Production and Exports," February 2001, and Helpman et al., "Export versus FDI," January 2003.

[71] Fillat-Castejón, Francois, and Wörz, "Cross-Border Trade and FDI in Services," February 2009, 10; 17; 20–21.

[72] Grünfeld and Moxnes, "The Intangible Globalization," 2003, 20–21.

[73] The remoteness variable has been calculated similarly in a number of previous studies. Often, the distance between i and bilateral trading partner j is excluded in the summation of all trading partners, m. Doing so would introduce only a slight change in the values of our remoteness variable due to the number of observations in our model. Anderson and Van Wincoop argue that remoteness has little explanatory power and should be replaced by a broader measure ("multilateral resistance") that accounts for the full range of differences in relative trade costs (Anderson and Van Wincoop, "Gravity with Gravitas," March 2003, 5–6). Baier and Bergstrand simplify this measurement using a Taylor-series expansion (Baier and Bergstrand, "*Bonus Vetus* OLS," 2009, 78–80). Both models require the strong assumption that trade costs are symmetric; that is, the cost of exporting from country i to j is approximately equivalent to the cost of exporting from country j to i. Even if the assumption does not hold for every pair of trading partners, the use of data that include bilateral trade flows can balance out the effects of any asymmetries. However, in our dataset, non-OECD countries appear solely as importers, so we do not have bilateral flows for many country pairs. Therefore, we proceed using the more traditional specification of remoteness.

[74] A random effects model allows one to estimate coefficients for variables that do not vary over time, such as SFDIR. Fixed effects and first differences, two other common methods for analyzing panel data, do not permit analysis of time-invariant variables. The random effects

model requires the assumption that the effects of any unobserved variables are uncorrelated with the independent variables in the model.

[75] The year dummies control for factors specific to those years that may have affected trade among all countries. OECD, OECD.Stat Extracts: Trade in Services by Partner Country Database (accessed August 2009).

[76] Ibid.

[77] The model does not capture such variables as more up-to-date policy indicators for Malaysia (i.e., the latest policy information is from 2004-05); economic growth within Malaysia; or the effects on the Malaysian service sector of trade preferences achieved through the implementation of free trade agreements.

[78] This figure includes banking, securities, and insurance services, though the latter are not covered in this report. Ministry of International Trade and Industry Malaysia, *Malaysia: International Trade and Industry Report 2007*, July 2008, 129.

[79] Bank Negara Malaysia, *Monthly Statistical Bulletin*, March 31, 2010.

[80] Official employment statistics of the Government of Malaysia do not disaggregate these sectors.

[81] Treasury Malaysia, *Economic Report 2009/2010*, November 2009.

[82] Bank Negara Malaysia, "The Financial Sector Masterplan," 2001.

[83] Ibid.

[84] EIU, *Country Finance: Malaysia*, 2006, 16; EIU, *Country Finance: Malaysia*, 2007, 3.

[85] EIU, *Country Finance: Malaysia* 2009, 14.

[86] EIU, Country Finance: Malaysia, 2007, 9–10.

[87] USTR, "Malaysia," 2008.

[88] EIU, *Country Finance: Malaysia*, 2007,16.

[89] Of the 17 Islamic banks in Malaysia, 11 are domestically owned, 3 are foreign owned but locally incorporated, and 3 are foreign owned. Bank Negara Malaysia, "List of Banking Institutions," May 31, 2008; EIU, Country Finance: Malaysia, 2009, 6.

[90] Bank Negara Malaysia, "Commercial Banks: Statement of Assets of Domestic and Foreign Banks" (accessed May 10, 2010).

[91] EIU, *Country Finance: Malaysia*, 2009, 11.

[92] Figure as of January 2010. Bank Negara Malaysia, "Commercial Banks: Statement of Assets of Domestic and Foreign Banks" (accessed May 10, 2010).

[93] Ibid.

[94] EIU, *Country Finance: Malaysia*, 2009, 14.

[95] USTR, "Malaysia," 2008.

[96] El-Gamal, *Overview of Islamic Finance*, August 2006, 4.

[97] Ibid., 7.

[98] Malaysia's central bank does not report data on Islamic banks' assets prior to December 2006. Bank Negara Malaysia, "Islamic Banking System, Statement of Assets (as of 31 January 2010)," (accessed March 23, 2010).

[99] Maybank Group, *Annual Report 2007*, September 7, 2007, 19, and *Annual Report 2009*, 2009, 58.

[100] Bumiputra-Commerce Holdings Berhad, *Annual Report 2007*, 2007, 157, and *Annual Report 2008*, 2008, 149.

[101] Public Bank Berhad, *Annual Report 2007*, 2007, 273, and *Annual Report 2009*, 2009, 363.

[102] Ministry of International Trade and Industry, Malaysia, *Malaysia: International Trade and Industry Report 2007*, July 2008, 139.

[103] USDOC, BEA, "U.S. International Services: Cross-Border Trade in 2008," October 2009, 50–52.

[104] Ibid.

[105] WTO, GATS, "Malaysia: Schedule of Specific Commitments," April 15, 1994, 47–65, and "Malaysia: Revised Offer," January 31, 2006, 32–35 and 39–40.

[106] WTO, "Trade Policy Review Report by the Secretariat: Malaysia," December 14, 2009, 61. For Islamic banks, the 70 percent foreign equity allowance applies only to existing institutions that plan to partner with foreign banks. Such banks must have capital reserves of no less than $1 billion in U.S. currency.

[107] Ibid., 59.

[108] Public institutions refer to government-owned or -subsidized facilities; private institutions are privately, or nongovernment, owned. Malaysian-German Chamber of Commerce and Industry, "Market Watch 2010," n.d.

[109] Yon, "Financing Health Care in Malaysia," 2004, 43–46.

[110] Danish Trade Council, Royal Danish Embassy, *The Health Care Sector,* March 31, 2009.

[111] Public hospitals include government hospitals, special medical institutions, and non-Ministry of Health government hospitals; private hospitals include maternity and nursing homes. Department of Statistics Malaysia also provides statistics on private facilities; however, there is some discrepancy between the numbers, as they cite 191 private hospitals and 67 private maternity homes. Comparable data are not available for clinics and other facilities. Ministry of Health (MoH), Malaysia, *Health Facts 2008,* May 2009; Danish Trade Council, Royal Danish Embassy, *The Health Care Sector*, March 31, 2009.

[112] USITC staff calculations based on data from MoH Malaysia, *Health Facts 2008,* 2009, and MoH, Malaysia *Health Facts 2004*, 2005.

[113] Average annual growth rate calculated by USITC staff using annual data from World Health Organization (WHO), "Malaysia," March 2010.

[114] USITC staff calculations based on data from WHO, "Malaysia," March 2010.

[115] WHO, "Malaysia," March 2010.

[116] Economic Planning Unit, Prime Minister's Department, *Ninth Malaysia Plan*, 2006, 435. Values converted from ringgit to dollars by USITC staff.

[117] The Seventh Malaysia Plan, enacted from 1996 through 2000, specified a move towards "the corporatization and privatization of hospitals as well as medical services" and a shift in government participation towards a regulatory role. Khoon, "Privatizing the Welfare State," 2003, 88.

[118] Danish Trade Council, Royal Danish Embassy, *Health Care Sector*, January 6, 2005; Leng, *Medical Tourism in Malaysia*, January 2007, 13.

[119] Values converted from ringgit to dollars by USITC staff a rate of 3.42 ringgit/dollar, the exchange rate as of January 4, 2010. International Monetary Fund, "Representative Exchange Rates for Selected Currencies for January 2010," n.d. (accessed January 4, 2010); Inland Review Board of Malaysia, "Tax Relief Summary: List of Tax Relief for Resident Individuals 2010," n.d. (accessed January 4, 2010); Yon, "Financing Health Care in Malaysia," 2004.

[120] Yong, "Tapping Into the Healthcare Services Sector in Malaysia," April 15, 2003, and Yon, "Financing Health Care in Malaysia," 2004.

[121] Ganesan, "Taking the Sting out of Medical Bills," March 10, 2007.

[122] USITC staff calculations based on Department of Statistics Malaysia, "Health Services (Private Sector)," November 3, 2009. In 2007 (the most recent year for which data are

available), general medical clinics and private hospitals accounted for over 80 percent of gross output in the private healthcare market.

[123] For 2003, the total number of establishments includes medical services and private hospitals and maternity homes. For 2007, the total number of establishments includes general medical clinics, specialty medical clinics, private hospitals, private maternity homes, and healthcare services. Statistics for healthcare services were not provided in 2003, general and specialist medical clinics were not broken out, and statistics for private hospitals and private maternity homes were summed together. Department of Statistics Malaysia, *Economic Census 2004 Malaysia—Health*, 2004, and "Health Services (Private Sector)," November 3, 2009.

[124] WHO, *Global Health Statistics 2008,* 2008.

[125] Danish Trade Council, Royal Danish Embassy, *The Health Care Sector*, January 6, 2005.

[126] Ministry of Health Malaysia, "Bahagian Telekesihatan (Telehealth Flagship Project)," n.d. (accessed June 19, 2008).

[127] Yong, "Tapping Into the Healthcare Services Sector in Malaysia," April 15, 2003; Meng, "The Briefing Session for Contract Doctors from the Arab Republic of Egypt," March 2, 2004.

[128] Department of Statistics Malaysia, "Number of Registered Medical Professionals by Ethnic Group—Malaysia," *Economic Census 2006 Malaysia – Health*, 2007.

[129] KPJ Healthcare Berhad Website, "Hospital Network," n.d. (accessed June 2008). (http://www.kpjhealth.com.my//index.php?option=com_content&task=view&id=168&Item id=139).

[130] Johor Corporation, "Corporate Profile," n.d. (accessed June 24, 2008).

[131] Arunanondchai and Fink, *Trade in Health Services in the ASEAN Region*, March 2007, 5.

[132] Columbia Pacific Healthcare is part of U.S.-based investment firm Columbia Pacific and operates hospitals throughout the region in India, Indonesia, Malaysia, and Vietnam. Columbia Asia Website. http://www.columbiaasia.com/index.html; Columbia Asia, "Columbia Asia Plans Aggressive Expansion in Malaysia," April 21, 2009.

[133] ParkwayHealth, "Global Presence," n.d. (accessed June 25, 2008).

[134] Ministry of International Trade and Industry Malaysia, "Industry Profile: Services: Healthcare," n.d. (accessed June 2008).

[135] Ahmad, *Healthcare Sector Overview*, September 26, 2001.

[136] Association of Private Hospitals Malaysia, cited in Malaysia-German Chamber of Commerce and Industry, "Market Watch 2010," n.d., 7. Values converted from ringgit to dollars by USITC staff the rate of 3.46 ringgits/dollar, the exchange rate as of December 31, 2008. International Monetary Fund, "Representative Exchange Rates for Selected Currencies for December 2008," n.d. (http://www.imf. org/external/np/fin/data/rms_ mth.aspx?SelectDate=2008-12-31&reportType=REP).

[137] Arunanondchai and Fink, *Trade in Health Services in the ASEAN Region*, March 2007, 3.

[138] Ibid., 6; Danish Trade Council, Royal Danish Embassy, *The Health Care Sector,* January 6, 2005.

[139] In 2002, a heart bypass procedure at an upscale private hospital cost $6,315 compared to $10,417 in Singapore and up to $90,000 in the United States. Business Monitor International, "Key Sectors," 2006, 46.

[140] Dewi, "Hospitals Set Fees for Health Tourism," October 28, 2003.

[141] Tax incentives offer a 70 percent income exemption for identified medical services, as well as for machines and equipment used in service provision. Leng, *Medical Tourism in Malaysia*, January 2007, 13; Ministry of Tourism Malaysia, "Tax Incentives," May 30, 2008 (accessed June 3, 2008).

[142] Leng, *Medical Tourism in Malaysia*, 13; Shaw, "Accreditation and ISO," 1997, 12; Tourism Malaysia, Advertising and Publicity Division, "Health Tourism in Malaysia," November 5, 2007. Certification by the International Standards Organization (ISO) is accreditation based on an industry model of international standards. In the services sector, general standards focus on the quality of processes rather than results. In the case of healthcare services, ISO attempts to reconcile "patients, population and scientific evidence." Leng, *Medical Tourism in Malaysia*, 13; Shaw, "Accreditation and ISO," 1997, 12; Tourism Malaysia, Advertising and Publicity Division, "Health Tourism in Malaysia," November 5, 2007.

[143] Joint Commission International (JCI), "Joint Commission International (JCI) Accredited Organizations," 2007, and "About Joint Commission International," JCI website. http://www.jointcommissioninternational.org/about-jci/ (accessed October 19, 2010). JCI works with global healthcare providers and government ministries of health to improve the safety of patient care. It has supplied accreditation, certification, education, and advisory services to healthcare organizations in more than 80 countries over the past 16 years.

[144] JCI, "JCI Accredited Organizations," 2010.

[145] Leng, *Medical Tourism in Malaysia*, January 2007, 11.

[146] Business Monitor International, "Key Sectors," 2006, 46.

[147] *The Sun*, "Pantai: Health Tourism to drive growth," September 15, 2004.

[148] *Islamic Finance News*, "Al-'Aqar KPJ REIT," n.d. (accessed June 24, 2008); Business Development Asia, "Malaysia," June 2007.

[149] *New Straits Times*, "Pantai to Expand Overseas Ops," December 7, 2004.

[150] Ibid.

[151] WTO, GATS, "Malaysia: Revised Offer," January 31, 2006, 63.

[152] WTO, "Trade Policy Review Report by the Secretariat, Malaysia," December 14, 2009, 56; *Tenth Malaysia Services Plan*, 2011–15, 122.

[153] Department of Statistics Malaysia, *Economic Census 2006: Transport and Communications*, December 2007, 99–167. Values converted from ringgits (RM 1.1 billion, RM 5.7 million, and RM 4.1 billion, respectively) to dollars by USITC staff.

[154] Exports require the ability to move cargo among sea, rail, and air carriers, and Malaysia's logistics sector has developed strong intermodal capacities.

[155] In turn, improvements in logistics infrastructure have attracted increased investment in Malaysia's exportoriented manufacturing sector.

[156] Malaysia Industrial Development Authority, "Malaysia's Growing Logistics Services," February 23, 2007. Values converted from ringgits (RM 46 billion and RM 35.8 billion respectively) to dollars by USITC staff.

[157] Tongzon, "Determinants of Competitiveness in Logistics," March 2007, 1.

[158] Bhatnagar, Jayaram, and Yue Cheng Phua, "Relative Importance of Plant Location Factors," March 2003, 154.

[159] Haq, "Halal Logistics Hits the Middle East," May 29, 2006.

[160] For example, halal and non-halal products cannot be stored in the same container.

[161] Ministry of International Trade and Industry Malaysia, "Official Portal of Ministry of International Trade and Industry Malaysia," n.d. (accessed July 2, 2008).

[162] Values converted from ringgits (RM 4.1 billion) to dollars by USITC staff.

[163] Ibid.

[164] Sohail, Bhatnagar, and Sohal, "A Comparative Study on the Use of Third Party Logistics Services by Singaporean and Malaysian Firms," November 2006, 694.

[165] Malaysia Industrial Development Authority, "Malaysia's Growing Logistics Service," February 23, 2007.

[166] American Association of Port Authorities, "World Ports Rankings, 2007," n.d. (accessed June 12, 2009).

[167] A TEU is the cargo capacity of one standard 20-foot long intermodal container; ports primarily handle cargo in the form of 20- and 40-foot containers.

[168] Portsworld.com Malaysia, "Record Performance by Malaysian Ports," February 11, 2008; Portsworld.com Malaysia, "Port Klang Authority," n.d. (accessed July 2, 2008); Ali, "Dubai-Based Operator Pulls Out of PKFZ," July 19, 2007. This port was privatized in 1986, with Port Klang Authority acting as a landlord, regulator, and trade facilitator. In 2004 Port Klang signed an agreement with Dubai's Jebel Ali Free Zone International (JAFZA) allowing them to manage the port, but in 2007 JAFZA withdrew from the concession, citing its inability to retain operational control as an equity stakeholder (Port Klang Authority had retained 100 percent of equity).

[169] Portsworld.com Malaysia, "Record Performance by Malaysian Ports," February 11, 2008; Mark, "Global Ambition," October 2007, 29. PTP has a deep, sheltered bay with a wide approach channel, and is capable of accommodating the *Emma Maersk* (the world's largest container ship, which can only dock at a handful of ports). It also has state-of-the-art cargo handling systems and IT infrastructure, as well as a dedicated airport code that lets airlines treat PTP as a flight destination. All of these investments have been partially underwritten by Denmark's Maersk Sealand and Taiwan's Evergreen Marine Corporation, which stand to benefit from the increased intermodal logistics capacity at Malaysian ports. The Pelepas Free Zone, established in 1998 to support export-oriented manufacturing facilities, includes PTP. In some cases, it is now cheaper for logistics firms to ship cargo to PTP, and then have it flown to China, than to ship directly to China.

[170] Portsworld.com Malaysia, "Record Performance by Malaysian Ports," February 11, 2008.

[171] American Association of Port Authorities, "World Port Rankings, 2007," n.d. (accessed June 12, 2009).

[172] Ibid.

[173] US&FCS and U.S. Department of State, "Doing Business in Malaysia," February 21, 2008.

[174] Mark, "Global Ambition," October 2007, 30.

[175] Putzger, "Searching for Space," March 2007, 38.

[176] Mark, "Global Ambition," October 2007, 30; Putzger, "MAS Momentum," June 2002, 20. The carrier was partially privatized in 1995, but the main stakeholder, Tajudin Ramli, eventually sold his 29 percent share back to the government.

[177] Putzger, "MAS Momentum," June 2002, 19.

[178] Putzger, "Grounded," September 2006, 44.

[179] Mark, "Global Ambition," October 2007, 30.

[180] Ibid. Goods are accepted only from registered shippers, all cargo is held for 24 hours and x-rayed before shipping, and U.S. customs officials make unannounced visits to monitor security.

[181] MASkargo, "Kargo Udara Mas," n.d. (accessed July 2, 2008).

[182] Treasury Malaysia, Ministry of Finance, *Economic Report 2007/2008*, 2008, 66.

[183] Mahmood, "Malaysia's Export Competitiveness in Services and the Third Malaysia Industrial Master Plan," October 8, 2007.

[184] Treasury Malaysia, Ministry of Finance, *Economic Report 2007/2008*, 2008, 65. Values converted from ringgits (RM 19.9 billion, RM 38.9 billion, and RM 19 billion respectively) to dollars by USITC staff.

[185] WTO, GATS, "Malaysia: Revised Offer," January 31, 2006, 67.

[186] WTO, "Trade Policy Review Report by the Secretariat, Malaysia," December 14, 2009, 56–7.

[187] *Airline Business*, "Asian Cargo Opens Up," April 2004.

[188] Ministry of International Trade and Industry Malaysia, "Official Portal of Ministry of International Trade and Industry Malaysia," n.d. (accessed July 2, 2008).

[189] US&FCS and U.S. Department of State, *Doing Business in Malaysia: 2008 Country Commercial Guide for U.S. Companies*, February 21, 2008.

[190] In 2005, 70 percent of life insurance premiums and 40 percent of general insurance premiums in Malaysia were written by foreign insurers.

INDEX

D

G

H

I

J

L

M

T